BUSINESS GOALS 2

STUDENT'S BOOK

Gareth Knight Mark O'Neil Bernie Hayden

CAMBRIDGE
UNIVERSITY PRESS

PUBLISHED BY THE PRESS SYNDICATE OF THE UNIVERSITY OF CAMBRIDGE
The Pitt Building, Trumpington Street, Cambridge, United Kingdom

CAMBRIDGE UNIVERSITY PRESS
The Edinburgh Building, Cambridge CB2 2RU, UK
40 West 20th Street, New York, NY 10011–4211, USA
477 Williamstown Road, Port Melbourne, VIC 3207, Australia
Ruiz de Alarcón 13, 28014 Madrid, Spain
Dock House, The Waterfront, Cape Town 8001, South Africa

http://www.cambridge.org

First published 2004

Printed in Italy by G. Canale & C. S.p.A.

Typeface Rotis Serif (Adobe Systems Incorporated) *System* QuarkXPress® [KAMAE]

A catalogue record for this book is available from the British Library

ISBN 0 521 75541 7 paperback

Contents

Map of the book

UNIT

1 Greeting visitors

UNIT GOALS • greeting visitors to your country • greeting visitors to your office • small talk

TALKING POINT

Have you met visitors to your company or country?
What do you offer them?
What do you talk about when you meet new people?
Do you find it easy or difficult to start a conversation?

PART A Greeting visitors to your country

1 Listening

a Jon Wright has travelled from England to Italy to visit one of his clients, a company called Planeta. Maria works for Planeta, and is meeting Jon at the airport. Which of these topics do you think they talk about?

1 Jon's flight ☐
2 Maria's family ☐
3 Maria's job ☐
4 politics ☐
5 the weather ☐
6 Jon's last holiday ☐
7 transport to the office ☐
8 the time it takes to get to the office ☐

b Listen to the conversation and tick (✓) the topics they mention.

2 Language focus

a Look at these expressions from the conversation in 1 Listening. **Who says them? Write H (for host) or V (for visitor).**

1 .... Thank you. That's very kind.
2 .... Can I help you with your bags?
3 .... Do you like travelling?
4 .... How long does it take to get there?
5 .... Do you travel abroad a lot?
6 .... I'm here to take you to our office.
7 .... No, it's all right, thanks. They're not heavy.
8 .... This way.
9 .... Did you have a good flight?
10 .... You can put your bags in the boot.

b Listen again and check your answers.

LANGUAGE FILE 1 >> **PAGE 86**

3 Language focus

Complete the sentences from 1 Listening **with the correct form of the verb in brackets.**

Example ....Did.... you ....have.... (have) a good flight, Mr Wright?

1 Yes, it .... (be) a good flight, and very short – I .... (not do) any work.

2 What .... you .... (do) at Planeta, Maria?

3 I .... (work) in Marketing now, but before that I .... (work) in Sales.

4 Right. Why .... you .... (change) departments?

5 One of the Marketing Assistants .... (leave), so I .... (apply).

LANGUAGE FILE 2 >> PAGE 87

4 Communication activity

a Work in pairs. Role play meeting a visitor at the airport.

Visitor	**Host**
Introduce yourself. →	Introduce yourself and greet your visitor. Ask about the flight.
Answer the host's questions. →	Offer to help with luggage.
Respond. Say something about the weather. →	Respond.
Ask how long it takes to get to the office. →	Answer the visitor's questions.

b Now change roles. Act out your role play for the class.

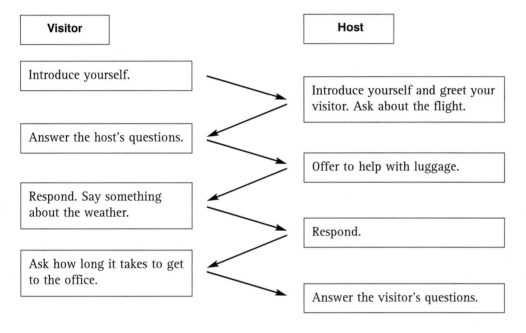

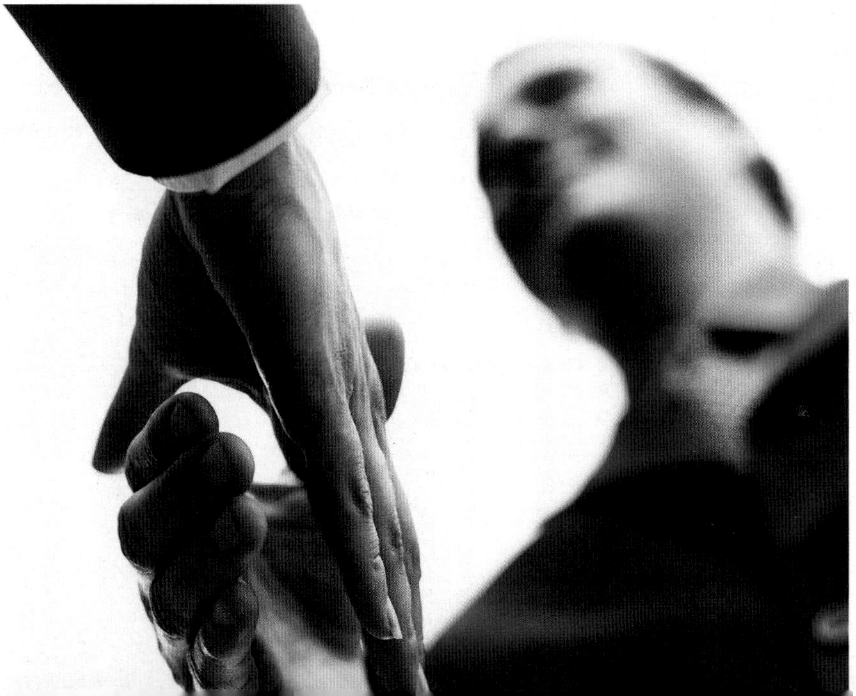

PART B Greeting visitors to your office

1 Culture focus

a When people meet in business, there is often 'small talk' before the business discussion begins. Read the tips for making small talk. Choose the three most important tips in your opinion.

b Compare your choices with a partner. Do any of the tips seem strange to you?

Making small talk in business

Talking easily with people can make a bigger impression than exchanging business cards. Here are some tips:

1. Smile first and always shake hands when you meet someone.
2. Take your time during introductions. Make an extra effort to remember people's names, and use them frequently in the conversation.
3. Maintain eye contact in any conversation.
4. Be aware of body language. Nervous people make others uncomfortable. Look confident and comfortable.
5. Be prepared. Think of three topics you can talk about.
6. Play the conversation 'game'. Answer with more than just 'yes' or 'no'.
7. Don't be a detective! Avoid all personal questions if you don't know the person well.

2 Listening

a Match the sentences 1–6 to the responses a–f.

1	Nice to meet you.	a	Not at all. Thank you for seeing me.
2	Hello. I'm Sonja Blum.	b	Nice to meet you, too.
3	Thank you for coming today.	c	Very well, thank you.
4	How are you?	d	Yes, please. That would be nice.
5	Would you like a coffee?	e	Hi, Steve Verwoert.
6	Hello. Nice to see you again.	f	Hello. Nice to see you, too.

b Which pairs of sentences would be used by people meeting for the first time? Which would be used by people who have met before? Which could be used by both? Complete the table.

First time	1 b
Met before	
Both	

c Listen to two conversations in which people greet each other. Which two people have met before and which haven't? How do you know?

3 Language focus

a Complete these sentences from 2 Listening**.**

1

CLAUDE: .... here before?
MICHAEL: Yes, well, ... to France before ...
CLAUDE: Oh, really? When .... that?
MICHAEL: Er, in 2003, I .... for the National Conference in Toulouse.
CLAUDE: Oh, yes, I .... to that.
MICHAEL: But I .... to Lyons before.

2

CATHY: Good. .... Tom before?
JENNY: Yes, ... Hello, Tom.
TOM: Hello, Jenny. I think we .... at last year's General Meeting.

b Listen again and check.

LANGUAGE FILE 3 >> **PAGE 87**

4 Communication activity

Work in pairs. You are going to greet visitors to your office.

Role play 1
You are meeting for the first time. Think about three topics you can talk about.

Host
Introduce yourself.
Offer your visitor a seat.
Offer your visitor a drink.
Make small talk.

Visitor
Introduce yourself.
Accept a drink.
Say 'thank you' when appropriate.
Make small talk.

Role play 2
You have met before and you know each other well. Think about three topics you can talk about.

Host
Greet your visitor. Ask how he/she is.
Offer a drink.
Make small talk.

Visitor
Greet your host and respond to his/her question.
Accept a drink.
Make small talk.

5 Exploring

a What is the right thing to do when you have meetings with visitors? Choose the answers about your company, or the answers which you think are best.

1 Where do you have meetings with visitors?
  a in the reception area
  b in a meeting room
  c at someone's desk

2 What do you offer visitors to drink?
  a a cold drink
  b a hot drink
  c a choice of hot or cold drinks

3 Do you offer visitors food?
  a yes, always
  b no, never
  c it depends on the time of day and the person

4 When do you have food?
  a before the meeting
  b during the meeting
  c after the meeting
  d never

b Compare answers in pairs. Do you think the answers are the same in all companies?

UNIT 2 Companies

UNIT GOALS • describing different kinds of company • giving profiles of companies

TALKING POINT

Think about your company or a company that you know.
What is the name of the company? What does it do?
Where is the company located? Is it international?

PART A Describing companies

1 Reading

a Read the text below and complete the labels for this diagram with words from the text.

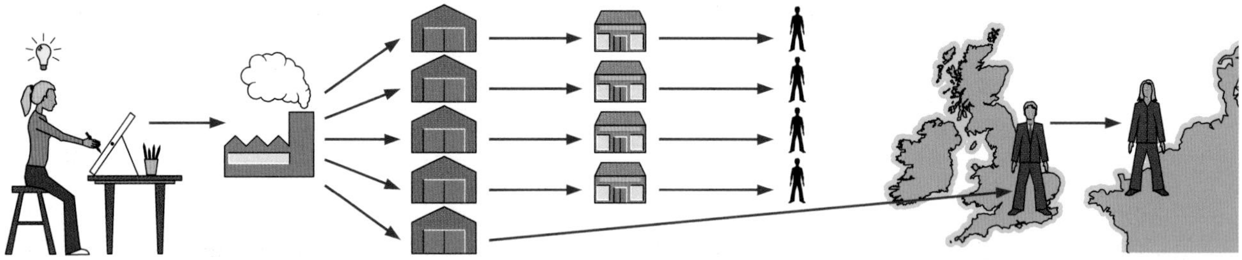

1	2	3	4	5	6	7
				customers		

I'm a designer. I think of new ideas for clothes for a manufacturer, who makes the clothes and sells them to wholesalers. They buy large quantities of the clothes, and sell them to different retailers, who sell clothes to individual customers in shops. Sometimes an exporter buys some clothes and sends them to other countries, where an importer buys them to sell in shops.

b Look at the following example:

I'm a **designer.** (person)
I **design** clothes. (verb)
I work in **design.** (area you work in)

Now complete the table.

Person/Company	Verb	Area
designer	design	design
		exports
importer		
	manufacture	
retailer		

VOCABULARY FILE 1 >> PAGE 89

2 Vocabulary

a Complete the sentences below with words from the box.

accountancy	car	clothes	computer	estate
furniture	insurance	law	ticket	travel

1 We are the biggest .... manufacturer in the region; we make more chairs and tables than anyone else.
2 We think it's best to use a big .... firm to help with the company finances.
3 Could you call the .... agent and book two seats for this evening's concert?
4 We have always used the same .... firm for legal advice; they are quite expensive, but very good.
5 I'm thinking of buying a new PC. Can you recommend a good .... dealer?
6 In this country, most people use an .... agent to buy or sell a house.
7 That .... manufacturer has a good contract with one of the big fashion stores.
8 After the fire in our office last year, the .... company paid for our new equipment very quickly.
9 We usually compare prices from two or three .... agents before we book flights and hotels.
10 Nowadays, ... manufacturers produce vehicles which are not so bad for the environment.

b Work in pairs. Can you think of any examples in your area of these kinds of companies?

Example *There's a big furniture manufacturer called Apex in my town.*

VOCABULARY FILE 2 >> PAGE 89

3 Listening

a Listen to radio advertisements for three different companies. Choose one phrase from the box to describe each company.

car dealer	law firm	clothes manufacturer	estate agent
ticket agent	insurance company		

1 SEATMASTER ....

2 GLOBE SPORTS ....

3 HAWES & Co ....

b Complete these sentences from the advertisements. Then listen again and check.

1 We .... London but we .... to businesses all over Europe.
2 We .... football kit.
We .... through our sales network.
3 Hawes and Company .... through the legal jungle of the modern business world.
We .... help and advice on all the legal aspects of your business.

4 Communication activity

STUDENT A: Look at the information on page 76.
STUDENT B: Look at the information on page 78.

PART B Company profiles

1 Reading

a Read the three company profiles below and complete the table.

	Where is it based?	When was it started?
Allen and Overy		
Relocations Asia–Pacific		
Ford Motor Company		

Allen and Overy, an international law firm with its Head Office in London, was established in 1930. The first overseas offices were opened in 1978 in Dubai and Brussels. It now has 26 branches in major centres around the world, where expert legal advice is offered in international capital markets, banking, property and corporate law. Our clients receive a personalized service to the highest international standards. In 1997 it was voted 'Best Global Law Firm'.

FORD MOTOR COMPANY is one of the world's largest vehicle manufacturers. It is based in Detroit, Michigan but has factories and distributors all over the world. Ford Motor Company was started in the early twentieth century by one man. Henry Ford developed products to meet the needs of people facing industrialization. Now, his ideas are developed by the company, as it designs and manufactures products to meet the changing needs of people in the global community.

Relocations Asia-Pacific specializes in sourcing high quality rental accommodation in Bangkok. Relocations was established 25 years ago, so our expert team has the experience to offer you a no-cost service in selecting houses or apartments in the location you want at the price you need. We believe in a highly personalized service and count many of our clients as friends.

b Read the profiles again and answer these questions.

1 What product or service does Allen and Overy offer?
2 When was Allen and Overy established outside the UK?
3 How many branches does Allen and Overy have?
4 What happened to Allen and Overy in 1997?
5 What product or service does Relocations Asia–Pacific offer?
6 How much does Relocations Asia–Pacific charge?
7 What is Relocations Asia–Pacific's philosophy?
8 Where does Ford Motor Company have factories?
9 What was Henry Ford's philosophy?
10 What is Ford Motor Company's philosophy today?

2 Language focus

a Complete the passive forms in these sentences from the company profiles.

1 Allen and Overy was established in 1930.

2 The first overseas offices .... in 1978 in Dubai and Brussels.

3 Expert legal advice ....

4 Relocations Asia–Pacific .... 25 years ago.

5 Ford Motor Company .... in the early twentieth century by one man.

6 Now, his ideas .... by the company.

b Make questions from the sentences above.

1 When was Allen and Overy established ?

2 Where .... in 1978?

3 What .... ?

4 When .... ?

5 When .... ?

6 What .... now?

LANGUAGE FILE >> PAGE 88

3 Communication activity

STUDENT A: **Look at the information on page 76.**
STUDENT B: **Look at the information below.**

a Use this information to answer Student A's questions about Airbus.

- established 1970
- Toulouse, France
- aircraft design and manufacture
- 46,000 employees
- annual turnover €19.4 billion
- 'setting the standards' = innovation, value, passenger comfort

b Student A has some information about Hitachi. Ask about Hitachi and make notes.

- when established?
- location?
- product/service?
- number of employees?
- annual sales?
- philosophy?

4 Writing

Write a short profile of the company you asked questions about in 3 Communication activity**.**

UNIT

3 Occupations

UNIT GOALS • talking about jobs • talking about responsibilities • talking about abilities

TALKING POINT

What job do you do, or would you like to do?
What do you need to do that job? Number these things from 1 (most important) to 6 (least important).

patience ☐ technical skills ☐ management experience ☐
qualifications ☐ confidence ☐ communication skills ☐

Tell your partner about the job.

PART A Describing your job

1 Vocabulary

Use words from each group to complete the table below, describing the jobs of the people in the photos.

Environment
laboratory
customers' offices
studio
call centre

Responsibility
quality control
finding new customers
dealing with customers' questions
brochure design

Job
graphic designer
engineer
customer service agent
sales representative

Job				
Environment				
Responsibility				

VOCABULARY FILE 1 >> **PAGE 91**

2 Listening

a Listen to two people talk about their jobs. Which of the people from 1 Vocabulary **are they?**

b Complete the table about the two people. Then listen again and check your answers.

Name:	Denise O'Connor	Derek Haslam
Works for:		
Likes job? Yes/No?		
Why?		

c Complete these things that Denise and Derek said. Then listen again and check.

1 I .... an advertising company in Dublin.

2 I .... all printed publicity material that the company produces.

3 It's .... that we give our clients the best printed advertising possible.

4 I .... an English toy company.

5 I'm .... safety testing, so it's .... that our toys are safe.

6 I .... a team of ten engineers.

LANGUAGE FILE 1 >> **PAGE 90**

3 Language focus

Read about the other two people in 1 Vocabulary **and answer the questions.**

1 When did Ron start working for Canon?

2 Does he work for them now?

3 When did Janine start working for HSBC?

4 Does she work for them now?

My name's Ron. I've worked for Canon since 1998. I'm a member of the sales team. It's my job to find new customers.

I'm Janine. I'm a customer service agent for HSBC. I've worked here for five years. I work in a call centre. I'm responsible for dealing with customers' questions.

LANGUAGE FILE 2 >> **PAGE 90**

4 Communication activity

STUDENT A: **Turn to page 77.** STUDENT B: **Look at the information below.**

a Imagine that you are Sam King. Prepare to tell Student A about your job.

	You	Your partner
Work for:	Fiat Cars – six years	
Job:	Production Manager – 2003 to now	
Environment:	Factory	
Responsibility:	Supervise paint process	

b Tell each other about your jobs, and complete the 'Your partner' column.

5 Exploring

Work in pairs. Tell each other about your work or studies. Then get into small groups and tell each other about your partner's work or studies.

PART B Talking about your abilities

1 Vocabulary

a Listen to Karen and Peter talking about a job advertisement and decide if these statements are true (T) or false (F).

1 Peter has the right experience for the job.

2 Peter thinks he can do the job easily.

3 Karen thinks he should apply for it.

4 Peter is definitely going to apply for it.

b Put these words which Karen and Peter used in the right groups below.

work under pressure	flexible	experience	creative
experienced	ambitious	good communication skills	work well in a team
organized	good computer skills	speak a foreign language	

be ...	have ...	be able to ...
flexible		

VOCABULARY FILE 2 >> PAGE 91

2 Language focus

a Complete the sentences with the words that Karen and Peter used in 1 Vocabulary. Then listen again and check.

1 You .... have at least three years' experience in marketing.

2 But you .... be experienced with tools.

3 You .... be flexible, creative, ambitious ...

4 .... be organized? I'm not!

5 But of course you .... have good communication skills.

6 And you .... be able to work well in a team and under pressure.

7 .... good computer skills.

8 .... speak any foreign languages?

9 I imagine you .... speak a foreign language.

10 Good, because I .... speak any languages apart from English.

b Work in pairs. Talk about the abilities you need to do these jobs.

office manager   teacher   TV reporter   scientist   writer

c Think about your job, or a job you would like to do. Talk to your partner about the abilities you need for that job.

LANGUAGE FILE 3 >> PAGE 90

3 Listening

a Work in pairs. Your company needs to send an employee to the Mexico City office to be Product Manager. What abilities and experience will that person need? Think of three things.

b With your partner, look at the personal histories of these three employees. Which one do you think is the best person? Why?

Example A: *I (don't) think Jeff should go / is best / would be good because ...*

B: *That's true / a good point, but maybe Chris is better because ...*

Anneliese Schulz

Nationality: German

Current position: Trainee Manager

Time with company: 1 year

Skills/experience: part of a team that introduced new targets system

Previous work experience: none

Qualifications: Master of Business Administration (MBA); Bachelor in International Business (BA)

Languages: German, English, Spanish

Jeff Talbot

Nationality: Canadian

Current position: Product Manager

Time with company: 3 years 6 months

Skills/experience: manages a large team; responsible for inter-group communications

Previous work experience: 1 year as engineer for Eriksson

Qualifications: Master of Management Information Systems (MS), Bachelor of Liberal Arts (BA)

Languages: English, French, Italian

Chris Barker

Nationality: British

Current position: Product Manager

Time with company: 22 years

Skills/experience: has managed teams in a number of different divisions; has given presentations at international conferences

Previous work experience: none

Qualifications: Bachelor of Economics

Languages: English

c Now listen to two senior managers talking about the three employees. Which of the things below did they consider? Which person did they choose? Do you agree with their decision?

- qualifications
- personality
- languages
- skills
- experience with the company
- experience with other companies
- knowledge of the country
- knowledge of the company and its products

4 Exploring

Do you think employers should consider any of these things when they select candidates for a job? Why / Why not?

- age
- nationality
- gender
- marital status
- number of children

Vocabulary 1

Complete the puzzle.

Across

1 An .... person has done something for a long time.

4 Sure about what you are doing.

6 Good at thinking of new ideas.

7 An .... person wants to be very successful.

9 Someone who has passed exams or courses is ....

Down

2 Never late.

3 Able to stay calm, especially when something takes a long time.

5 Able to change depending on the situation.

8 A teacher needs good communication ....

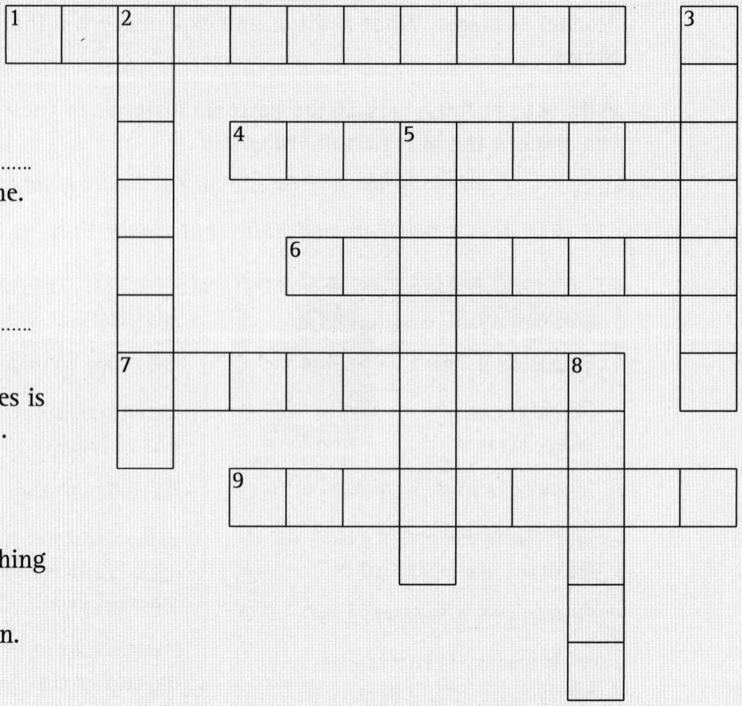

Language 1

Isabella is meeting Clare at the airport. Put their conversation in the correct order.

a Hello. Are you Clare Jones? [1]

b It takes about an hour by car. Is this your first time in Rome? [ ]

c I'm Isabella. We spoke on the phone. [ ]

d Yes. Actually, it's my first time in Italy. [ ]

e Oh, really? How was your flight? [ ]

f Yes, that's right. Hello. [ ]

g Nice to meet you, too. Can I take one of those bags? [ ]

h Oh, not too bad. Just a slight delay at Heathrow. [ ]

i Thank you. Is it far to your office? [ ]

j Yes. It's good to meet you at last. [ ]

Now practise the conversation with a partner.

Communication 1

With a partner, role play the following situations.

Situation 1

STUDENT A: You are meeting Student B at the airport. You know each other quite well. Greet each other and make small talk.

STUDENT B: You have just arrived in Student A's country. You know each other quite well but this is your first time in this country. Make small talk.

Situation 2

STUDENT A: You have just arrived at Student B's company for a meeting. It is the first time you have met. Greet each other and make small talk as you go to a meeting room.

STUDENT B: You are meeting Student A at the reception desk in your company. It is the first time you have met. Greet each other and make small talk as you go to a meeting room.

Vocabulary 2

Choose the right words to make compound nouns.

1 accountancy *manufacturer / firm*

2 car *dealer / agent*

3 clothes *dealer / company*

4 estate *agent / firm*

5 furniture *dealer / firm*

6 insurance *firm / manufacturer*

7 law *dealer / firm*

8 ticket *agent / dealer*

Work in pairs. Decide which companies above these people should go to.

1 We'll need to get some new vehicles soon.

2 I'd like to see if we can find a bigger office closer to the centre.

3 Shall we take our visitors out to see a show on Friday?

4 I need someone to check that I've got these finances right.

5 This is a complex legal problem – I think we need professional advice.

6 We haven't got enough desks for the staff who are moving here next month.

Language 2

Complete the text with the correct forms of the verbs in brackets.

My name's Jason and I (1) .... (work) for a big car company called Lord. I (2) .... (be) very happy in my work; I (3) .... (like) it very much. I (4) .... (start) at their north-east branch six years ago, then I (5) .... (move) to Head Office by the company. I (6) .... (be) at Head Office for just a month, and at the moment they (7) .... (train) me to be a manager. I (8) .... (not enjoy) the training so much, but I'll earn more money in the new job!

Communication 2

Think of a job you would *not* like to do. Tell your partner what skills and abilities you need to do the job, and why you wouldn't like it.

UNIT

4 Products

UNIT GOALS
- talking about office equipment
- describing the features and benefits of products

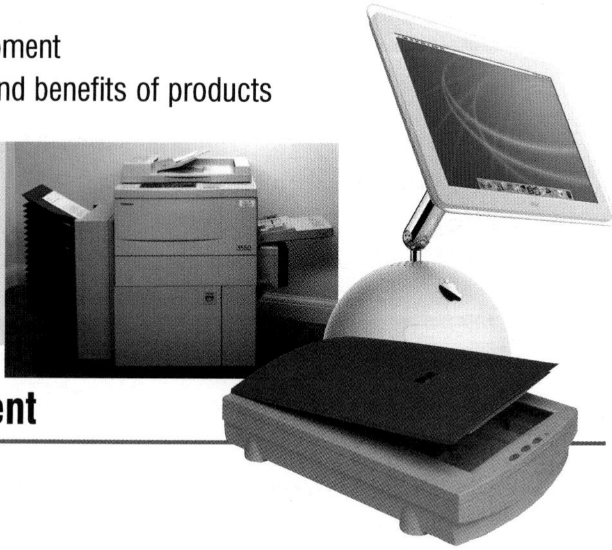

TALKING POINT

What equipment is used in an office?
What problems can people have with office equipment?
Is it best to buy equipment that is cheap, easy-to-use or attractive?

PART A Talking about office equipment

1 Vocabulary

Match the adjectives 1–8 to their opposites a–h.

1 fast	5 modern/up-to-date	a unreliable	e slow
2 light	6 quiet	b unattractive/ugly	f old-fashioned/out-of-date
3 reliable	7 flexible	c noisy	g complicated
4 simple/easy-to-use	8 attractive	d inflexible	h heavy

VOCABULARY FILE >> PAGE 93

2 Language focus

a Complete the complaints about a computer with these adjectives.

modern   old-fashioned

1 It's *too* .... (*too* + adjective)
2 It's *not* .... *enough*. (*not* + adjective + *enough*)

old-fashioned

b Work in pairs. Make two similar sentences about each of these things.

1 old

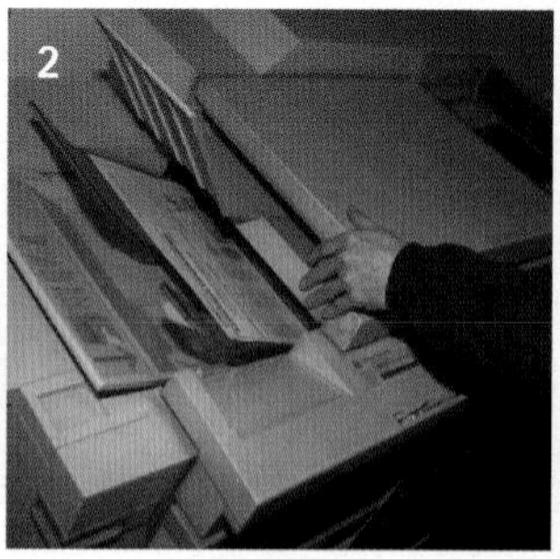

2 slow

3 noisy

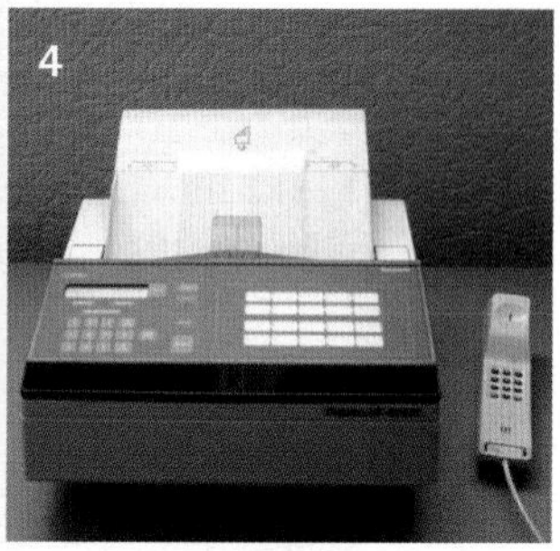

4 unreliable

c Now tell your manager what you need, and why. Use *so* and *because*.

Examples *My mobile phone's too old so I need a new one.*
We need a new photocopier because this one's too slow.

LANGUAGE FILE 1 >> PAGE 92

3 Listening

a Listen to an Office Manager telling a Facilities Manager what his office needs, and complete columns 1 and 2 of the table.

	1 What do they need?	2 Why do they need it?	3 Comparative
1		The one they've got is too	Right, I'll check the cost of a .... machine.
2		The ones they've got aren't .... enough.	OK, I can find out about .... desks.
3		The old one is too	Is it possible to get a .... one?

b Listen again and complete column 3 of the table.

c Look at the pictures and think of some problems you might have with these things. With your partner, take turns to explain what is wrong with the equipment and why you need a new one. Use *too/enough* and the comparative form of adjectives.

1
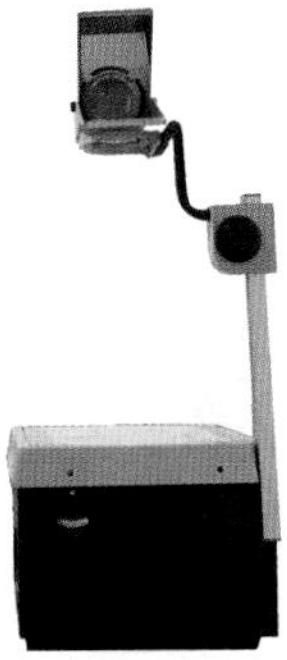

2
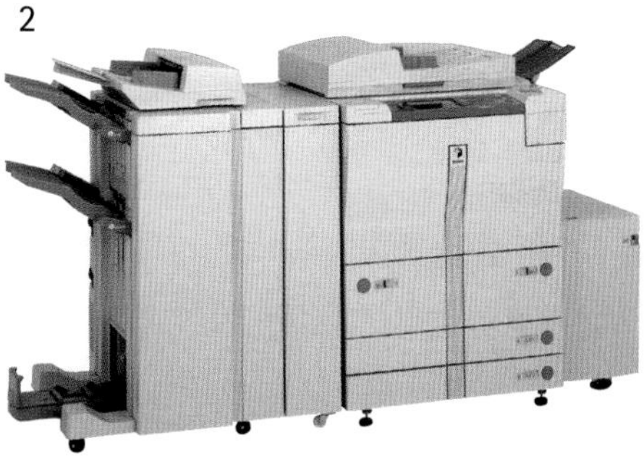

3

4

5

6

4 Communication activity

a Think of one thing you need for your office. Write down what you need, and some reasons why you need it.

b Work in groups. You each need something new for your office, but your company only has enough money for one thing. You should each explain what you need, and why. Then the group should decide which piece of equipment to buy, and why.

c Explain your decisions to the class.

PART B Talking about features and benefits

1 Listening

a Listen to the beginning of a training session and complete the definitions.

1 Features are the .... a product.

2 The benefits are why .... the customer.

b Now listen to the trainer talking about the features of software for presentations. Number these features in the order they are mentioned.

a attractive ☐	c flexible ☐	e fast ☐
b easy-to-use ☐	d reliable ☐	f up-to-date ☐

c Match the features above to these benefits. Then listen and check your answers.

1 You can use it with most modern computers. ☐

2 It won't stop working in the middle of your presentation. ☐

3 Your audience won't have to wait for each image to appear. ☐

4 You don't have to spend long learning how to use it. ☐

5 You'll create a good impression with your audience. ☐

6 You can easily change things when you're preparing. ☐

2 Language focus

Listen to the trainer again and complete these sentences.

1 This .... that you .... create great presentations straight away.

2 You .... spend hours learning how to use it.

3 It's up-to-date, which .... use it with most modern computers.

4 You .... things when you're preparing.

5 You .... wait a long time for each image to appear.

LANGUAGE FILE 2 >> PAGE 93

3 Reading

a These four people each have to give a presentation and they need to choose what equipment to use. Read about what they want.

1 **Shane Hooper** wants to prepare everything before the presentation. He isn't confident with computers and hasn't got time to learn now! He doesn't want to carry anything heavy because he is travelling by train.

2 **Paola Mirelli** wants to prepare everything in advance. She needs to present a lot of graphs and tables. She likes technology, and she has a car so she doesn't mind taking equipment.

3 **Eva Lozowski** wants to write ideas from participants during her presentation for everyone to see, and keep a written record to take away. She doesn't want to carry anything big or heavy.

4 **Joe Matthews** wants to note down ideas during the presentation but he doesn't need to keep a record. He doesn't want to carry anything heavy.

b Now read about four different types of presentation equipment opposite and decide which is the best one for each person.

presentationsolutions

Mobile flipchart

Features

▲ Large area, with extending arms
■ Adjustable height
● Wheels

Benefits

▲ You will be able to write a lot before turning to a new page.
■ This enables you to keep the chart at a comfortable height for you.
● You can move the flipchart around easily; you don't have to carry it.

Portable overhead projector

Features

▲ Small and very light, with integrated case
■ High output lamps and lens
● Twin lamps

Benefits

▲ This enables you to carry it easily to different locations.
■ This means it will always produce a clear, bright image that is easy to see.
● You don't need to worry if one lamp fails, because you can change to the other one.

Dry-wipe whiteboard

Features

▲ Large area
■ Dry wipe
● Easy to clean

Benefits

▲ You can write a lot and keep it clear and easy to read.
■ You don't need to use special board cleaners, or wet cloths.
● You will always be able to start with a clean board and present a professional image.

Presentation software

Features

▲ Easy-to-use
■ Many different templates
● High quality colours and graphics

Benefits

▲ You don't need to spend a long time learning how to use it.
■ This enables you to create just the presentation you need.
● You will be able to give a professional and memorable presentation.

4 Exploring

In groups, discuss these questions.

1 What are the disadvantages of each of the four types of equipment in 3 Reading?

2 Which one do you / would you prefer to use for presentations? Why?

UNIT

5 Comparing services

UNIT GOALS • talking about business services • comparing services • expressing your opinion, agreeing and disagreeing

TALKING POINT

Which of these services do businesses use most frequently?

- parcel delivery
- car hire
- stationery supplies
- banking services
- airlines
- catering

Do you know any companies that provide these services?

PART A Business services

1 Reading

a Work in pairs. Discuss which of these things are most important when choosing a service.

speed   price   convenience   reliability

b What are the adjectives, and their opposites, from the nouns above?

c Read the adverts for parcel delivery companies and answer the questions.

Which company is …

1 the fastest?

2 the cheapest?

3 the most convenient?

Delivery force
A4 size from 35
Guaranteed next-day delivery
(Bring your item to one of our offices before 4.00 p.m.)
Most deliveries before 12 noon in major cities
Tel: 354 5676

NTN Express
1-day, 2-day or 3-day service to any country in Europe
We guarantee the cheapest price!
Call now: 986 9834

Royal Star
We collect and deliver documents door-to-door
Guaranteed next-day delivery before 10.00 a.m.
3-day economy service also available
Prices start at 90

d Ben wants to send a very important document to a customer in Austria. It must arrive before 12 noon the next day. Which service should he use? Why? Discuss with a partner.

LANGUAGE FILE 1 >> PAGE 94

2 Listening

Ben is talking to his colleague Judy about which delivery service to use – Delivery Force or Royal Star. Listen and tick (✓) the boxes in the table.

	Delivery Force	Royal Star
cheaper		
safer		
Ben's choice		

3 Language focus

a Complete Judy's sentences from 2 Listening**.**

1 Delivery Force are .... good.

2 Royal Star are .... expensive!

3 Delivery Force are .... cheaper.

b Listen again and check your answers.

c Which sentences in (a) above can these words go into?

extremely a bit fairly a lot quite

LANGUAGE FILE 2 >> PAGE 95

4 Communication activity

STUDENT A: **Look at the information on page 77.**
STUDENT B: **Look at the information below.**

Situation 1

You need 50 full-colour brochures for a presentation to an important client in two days, and 100 black and white leaflets for a staff training session next week. Ask Student A to recommend a good printing company. Talk to Student A and fill in the table. Then tell Student A which you think is better, and why.

	Price	Quality	Speed
Multiprint			
Budget Print			

Situation 2

Student A wants you to recommend a conference facility. Most of the participants will be arriving by train. Tell Student A about the conference facilities below (price, size, convenience).

Example

Event Management Ltd has the largest rooms, for 200 people, but the Northern Hotel is the cheapest. Park Hotel is more convenient than ...

Park Hotel
Conference room available
For groups of up to 150 people
Just 180 per hour
10 minutes' walk from
Melville Town Station

Event Management Ltd
Conference Centre
Large rooms for 200 people or more
500 per hour
Opposite Melville Town Station
Tel: 04 467 0101

Northern Hotel
Three conference rooms available
Max. 30 people – 80 per hour
Max. 50 people – 120 per hour
Max. 100 people – 150 per hour

PART B Expressing your opinion

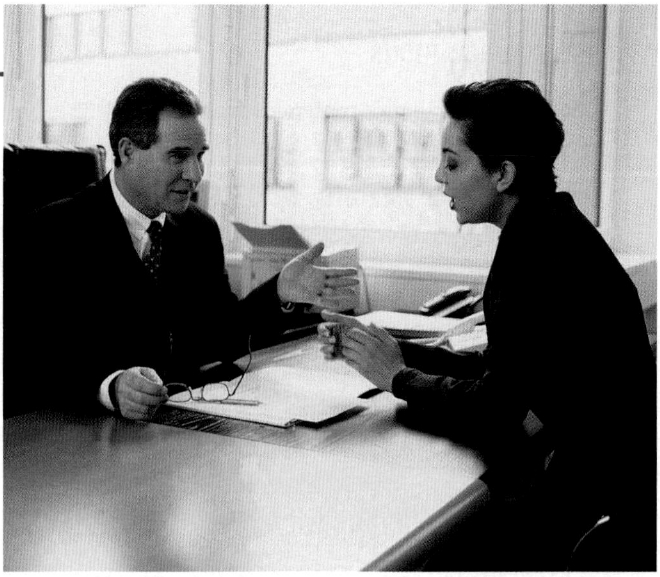

1 Listening

a Two managers of a business school want to add a new course to their programme. They are discussing ideas. Listen and put these ideas in the correct columns in the table below.

1 Employees can use them all the time at work.
2 All businesses use them.
3 It's very good for the company.
4 Employees might not think it's useful.
5 There's a very big market.
6 A lot of people don't need a training course.

Computer skills		Time-management skills	
Advantages	Disadvantages	Advantages	Disadvantages

b Can you add any more ideas to the table?

2 Language focus

a Complete these sentences with the expressions which the managers used in 1 Listening.

1 I .... a computer course is best. ☐
2 I .... , but a lot of people can already use them. ☐
3 If .... , a time-management course is best. ☐
4 I .... , but I .... employees will think it's very useful. ☐
5 Good .... – I .... that. ☐
6 Yes, ... Let's see what they think. ☐

b Listen again and check.

c For each of the expressions above, decide if the managers are:

a giving a opinion b agreeing completely c agreeing, but not completely.

d Work in pairs. Discuss which course you think is best, and why.

LANGUAGE FILE 3 >> PAGE 95

3 Writing

Work in pairs. Your company wants to send its staff on a training course. You think a time-management course is the best idea. You have received this email from a colleague. Write a reply.

to: you@yourcompany.com
from: rdavies@yourcompany.com
subject: Training courses

I don't think we should send our staff on a time-management course. It's very expensive, and if you ask me, there are more important things that they need to learn, like computer skills and telephone skills. What do you think?

Roger

4 Communication activity

Your company works to send the staff on a training course. Look at the different courses below, and think about the advantages and disadvantages of each one.

Team-building – residential
Friday 3 p.m. to Sunday 6 p.m.

Telephone skills – at your office
One session – Monday 9 a.m.–1 p.m.

Computer skills – at our college
Three sessions – Wednesday 2 p.m.–6 p.m.

Business letter writing – at our college
Four sessions – Monday 2 p.m.–4 p.m., Thursday 7 p.m.–9 p.m.

Finance – at your office
Two full days – Friday 9 a.m.–5 p.m.

Work in groups. Discuss the different courses and decide which one is best for your staff.

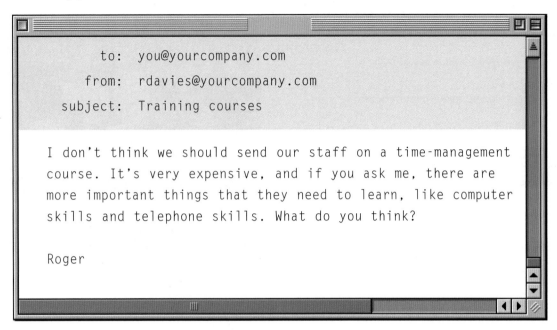

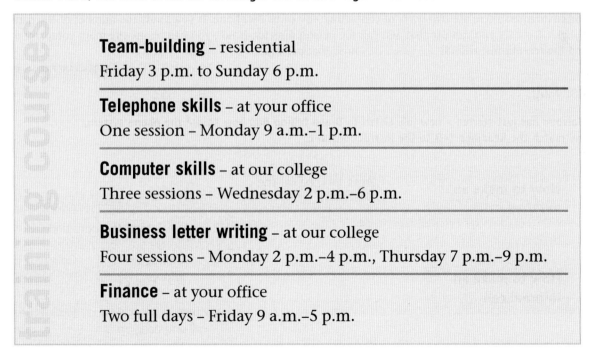

UNIT

6 Office systems

UNIT GOALS
- explaining how to use communication technology
- talking about systems and procedures in the office

TALKING POINT

What would you be worried about when starting a new job?
What office equipment do you need to learn how to use?

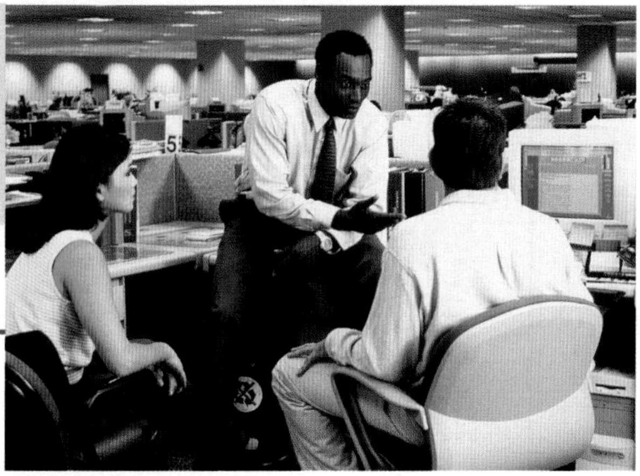

PART A Everyday office technology

1 Vocabulary

Complete the texts below, using the words in the box.

extension	external call	internal call	outside line
transfer	dialling tone	direct line	engaged/busy

For employees: To make an (1) .... (to someone outside the company), first listen for the (2) .... Next, press the EXT button to get an (3) .... , then dial the number of the person you want to call. To make an (4) .... (to someone within the company), you just need to call that person's (5) .... If the line is (6) .... , you should wait a few minutes and then try again.

For customers: There are two ways of contacting any of us by phone. If you know the number of the person's (7) .... , you can use that and call the person directly. If not, you can phone the main company number, and the receptionist will (8) .... you to that person.

VOCABULARY FILE >> PAGE 97

2 Listening

Malcolm has just started a new job. Listen to Diana telling him how to use the phone system, and match the headings 1–3 to the instructions a–c.

1 **How to make an external call**

2 **How to make an internal call**

3 **How to transfer an outside caller to a colleague**

a Press INT. » Dial the extension.

b Press INT.
» Dial the extension.
» [Colleague answers.] » Say there is an external call and hang up.
» [Colleague doesn't answer.] » Press INT to return to caller.

c Press 9. » Wait for a dialling tone. » Dial the number.

3 Language focus

a Complete these sentences from 2 Listening**.**

1 .... you want to make an internal call, press INT.

2 .... you want to make an external call, press 9.

3 .... you hear the dialling tone, dial the number.

4 .... the phone rings, just answer it.

5 .... your colleague answers, explain that there's an external call, and hang up.

6 .... your colleague doesn't answer, press INT to return to the outside caller.

b Listen again and check.

LANGUAGE FILE 1 >> PAGE 96

4 Communication activity

STUDENT A: **Look at the information on page 78.**
STUDENT B: **Look at the information below.**

a Listen to Student A explain how to use an office voicemail system. Make notes.

b Now explain to Student A how to set up an email holiday message. Use *if* or *when* and the prompts below to help you. Student A will make notes.

1 Want to leave email holiday message → No – shut down, have a good holiday! / Yes – open mail management screen.

2 Five options appear on screen → Click on 'holiday message'.

3 Computer asks you to log in → Enter username and password.

4 Want to write own message → Yes – click 'yes', type message, click 'enter'. / No – click 'no' for standard message.

5 See mail management screen → Click 'exit' – shut down, have a good holiday!

5 Exploring

Work in pairs. Choose one of the tasks below and write instructions on how to do it.

- saving a document on a computer
- sending a fax
- using a photocopier
- using a cash machine

When you are ready, explain your instructions to the class.

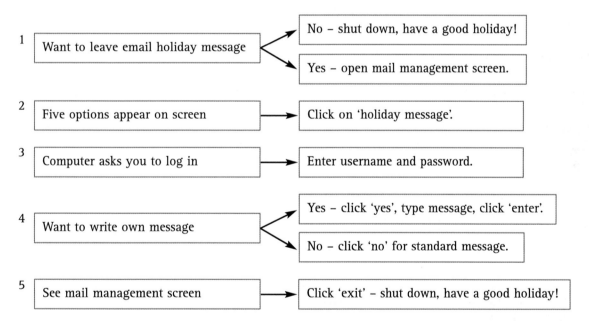

PART B Company procedures

1 Reading

a Read these instructions for a travel agent's booking procedure, and put the notes below in the right order.

TELEPHONE FLIGHT ENQUIRIES
When you take a flight enquiry, first ask when and where the customer wants to travel. Before you check flight availability, ask how many adults, children and infants are travelling. Check flight availability and once you have found an available flight, make a provisional reservation. After you have checked that the customer is happy with the flights, take the customer's details – name, address, phone number, credit card – and confirm the reservation. As soon as the tickets arrive, check that they are correct, then post them to the customer.

a Ask about number of passengers.
b Check tickets and post to customer.
c Ensure customer is happy with the flight.
d Check for available flights.
e Make provisional reservation.
f Confirm reservation.
g Take customer's personal details.
h Ask for dates and destinations.

b Find five time expressions in the text above which connect actions.

Example <u>When</u> *you take a flight enquiry, ...*

LANGUAGE FILE 2 >> PAGE 96

2 Listening

Neil, a new employee at the travel agent's in 1 Reading, has some questions for Tonya, his manager. Listen to their conversation and complete the table.

	Question	Yes/No?	Why?
1	Exact number of passengers necessary?		
2	Preferred airline important?		
3	Phone number important?		
4	Credit card necessary?		
5	Always post tickets to customer?		

3 Language focus

Complete Neil's questions below with the expressions in the box. Then listen to the conversation again and check.

I wasn't sure if	I think you mentioned	just one last thing	Another thing
did you say that	just clarify what you said	can I just check	

1 Yes, most of it. But .... a few things with you?

2 Well, first, ... we need the exact number of passengers before we check availability?

3 OK, fine. .... was, ... we should ask customers if they have a preferred airline.

4 Right. And .... taking the customer's phone number – is that really important?

5 What about credit cards? Can I .... about that?

6 OK, thanks. And .... – do we always post tickets to customers?

LANGUAGE FILE 3 >> PAGE 97

4 Communication activity

a **Work in pairs. This company sells sports equipment. The pictures below show the procedure for taking a telephone order. Put the pictures in the correct order.**

a

packing goods

b

taking card details

c

answering the phone

d

posting goods

e

entering the order in the system

f

selecting items from stock

b **Now change pairs. One student describes the procedure, the other makes notes. Then imagine it's the next day. Use your notes to ask questions to clarify the information.**

5 Writing

Work in pairs. Write brief instructions for an office procedure manual, either for your own office, or for the procedure in 4 Communication activity.

REVIEW 2

Vocabulary 1

Find the opposites of these adjectives in the puzzle.

slow   old-fashioned   out-of-date   unreliable
complicated   heavy   noisy   inflexible

R	B	N	F	A	S	T	I	O	W
C	Z	L	L	N	I	N	T	F	S
Q	U	I	E	T	M	U	C	G	A
U	N	E	X	O	P	P	L	A	B
I	D	L	I	G	H	T	D	E	M
C	E	A	B	L	V	O	F	J	O
F	N	N	L	E	E	D	X	A	D
I	L	R	E	L	I	A	B	L	E
M	O	D	E	F	A	T	O	O	R
C	S	I	M	P	L	E	V	A	N

Now write the comparative form of each adjective you found in the puzzle.

Example fast → *faster*

Language 1

Complete each sentence below in two ways, using *too* and *not ... enough.*

Example
I need a new PC because this one is too slow / not fast enough . (slow/fast)

1 My mobile phone is .... so I'm going to order a new one. (old-fashioned/modern)

2 I need newer software because this version is .... (old/up-to-date)

3 My company's location is .... , so we're going to move. (convenient/incovenient)

4 Please don't use ABC Couriers; they're .... (reliable/unreliable)

5 Can we get a new photocopier? This one is .... (complicated/simple)

Communication 1

Think about a piece of equipment that you use a lot. Make notes about some of the features and benefits.

Example

Mobile phone

Features	*Benefits*
large phone book	*stores a lot of numbers*
small	*can fit in your pocket*

Work in pairs. Imagine you are trying to sell your piece of equipment to your partner. Tell him/her about the features and benefits, and answer any questions your partner asks you.

Example
A: *This mobile phone has a large phone book, so you can store a lot of phone numbers.*
B: *Is it light to carry?*

Vocabulary 2

Work in pairs. Match the two parts of the sentences.

1 My phone rang, but when I picked up
2 I haven't got Jo's direct line number,
3 My redial button isn't working, so if a
4 The operator took so long to transfer me
5 To get an outside line, press '0',

a so I'll have to call the switchboard.
b that I gave up waiting and hung up.
c then wait for a dialling tone.
d the receiver, there was nobody there.
e line's busy, I have to dial the whole number again.

Language 2

Look at the instructions on the right for using a scanner and choose the correct words in the text below.

(1) *Before / After* you open the scanner program, check that your document is the right size and that the quality is good enough to scan. (2) *If / When* you see the words 'insert document' on the screen, open the lid and put the document in. (3) *If / Once* you want to scan a colour document, click on the colour icon. (4) *As soon as / If* your document is black and white, click on the black and white icon. (5) *Once / Before* the lamp has warmed up click on 'scan'. (6) *If / As soon as* the scanner finishes, click on the document and save it.

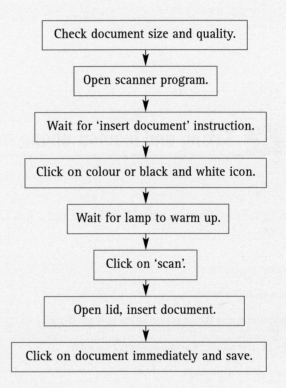

Check document size and quality.
↓
Open scanner program.
↓
Wait for 'insert document' instruction.
↓
Click on colour or black and white icon.
↓
Wait for lamp to warm up.
↓
Click on 'scan'.
↓
Open lid, insert document.
↓
Click on document immediately and save.

Communication 2

Work in groups. Discuss the different training courses below. Try to decide which one is the most important and which one is the least important.

presentation skills	handling budgets	effective meetings
team-building	using the Internet	managing stress

Example

A: *I think handling budgets is the most important as the company needs to make a profit.*

B: *That's true, but not everyone in the company works with budgets. If you ask me, a team-building course would be better because that involves everyone.*

A: *I see what you mean, but ...*

UNIT

7 Phone messages

UNIT GOALS
- answering the phone and taking messages
- leaving phone and voicemail messages

TALKING POINT

How often do you take/leave phone messages?
How do you feel about ...
... taking/leaving phone messages in your language / in English?
... leaving voicemail messages in your language / in English?

PART A Taking and leaving phone messages

1 Listening

Listen to Tony Markham making three phone calls. Tick (✓) the things that happen in each call.

	Call 1	Call 2	Call 3
1 Tony gives his name.			
2 The person who Tony wants to speak to is not there.			
3 The person who Tony wants to speak to is there.			
4 Tony leaves a message.			
5 Tony says he will call later.			
6 Tony spells his surname.			

2 Language focus

a Match the expressions 1–6 from 1 Listening to those with a similar meaning a–f.

1 Can I have your name, please?
2 Just a moment, please.
3 I'll put you through.
4 This is Tony Markham.
5 His line's busy right now.
6 Would you like to leave a message?

a Can you hold, please?
b He's on another call at the moment.
c Can I take a message?
d May I ask who's calling?
e Tony Markham speaking.
f I'll connect you.

b Look at the Transcript on page 121 and practise the conversations in pairs. Take turns to be Tony and the receptionist.

LANGUAGE FILE 1 >> PAGE 98

3 Listening

a **Listen to two phone calls and complete the messages.**

1

MESSAGE	
For:	
Call from:	
Time:	4.20 p.m.
Call back ___ Will call again ___	
Message:	
Number:	

2

While you were out ...	
Message for:	
______ called	
at	10.00 a.m./~~p.m.~~
Message:	
Number:	

b **Look at the Transcript on page 121 and practise the conversations in pairs. Take turns to be the caller and the receptionist.**

4 Exploring

Look at the four situations below, where a receptionist answers and says that the person called is not available. In pairs, discuss the best thing for the caller to do (a, b or c) in each of the situations.

1 Peter calls a colleague, Gemma, to tell her about a report he has written. Gemma is not in the office today.

2 Nicola Hancock is planning to come to a meeting at Pam Coleman's office. Pam calls her to find out what time her flight is going to arrive, but she is in a meeting.

3 Niall Rogers has complained to Sandra Hoffman about some items missing from his order. Sandra has arranged for the items to be delivered tomorrow. Sandra calls to tell Niall this, but he is on the phone to someone else.

4 Martina Lopez is preparing some information for her company's brochure, but she is not sure about the latest prices. Martina calls Paco, the Sales Manager, to ask him but he is out of the office today.

a Leave a message explaining everything.

b Ask the receptionist to get the other person to call back.

c Leave a message about the general situation but send the details in an email.

5 Communication activity

With a partner, role play the conversations in 4 Exploring**. Change roles after each conversation. When you are the receptionist, write down any message that the caller leaves.**

PART B Leaving voicemail messages

1 Reading

a Work in pairs. Discuss these statements about making phone calls. Which ones do you think are good advice?

1 Make a note of the things you want to talk about.

2 Phone at lunchtime.

3 If the other person already knows you, don't say your name.

4 If you get through to someone's voicemail, don't leave a message.

5 Say the name of your company in a message.

6 Just leave a short message.

b Read this advice about making phone calls and check your answers.

Before you call ...

Think about your main reason for calling, and what you want to say. Make a list of things to say before you call, so that you don't forget anything while you are on the phone. You could also try to imagine the other person's answers, so that you can be prepared.

Try to choose a good time to phone. It's not usually a good idea to phone very early or very late in the working day, or around lunchtime. And if you call another country, think about what time it is in that country.

When you call ...

If the other person is available, say who you are (he/she may not recognize your voice) and briefly why you are calling – give him/her time to remember the topic, as he/she is probably not thinking about it when you phone.

Leaving a message ...

If the other person isn't there and you have to leave a message, remember to say:

- your name and the name of your company – spell any difficult words.
- your telephone number – you may want to give a different number, for example a mobile, if you know you will be out.
- the best times/days to contact you.
- why you called.
- what you want the other person to do, for example call you back.

Keep your message short and clear – just give the minimum necessary information. If you need to say more, it may be better to email, and refer to your email in the phone message.

c Discuss the advice about leaving a message. Are there any situations in which some of the advice wouldn't be necessary?

2 Listening

Listen to three voicemail messages. Tick (✓) the things each listener should do.

	Listener 1	Listener 2	Listener 3
call back			
send an email			
check their email			
send a brochure			
visit the caller			
expect another call			

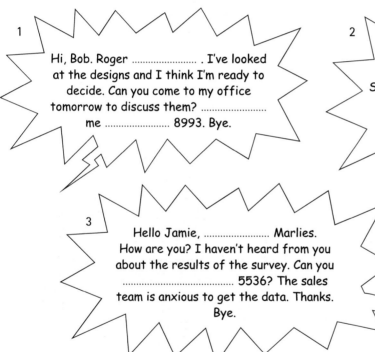

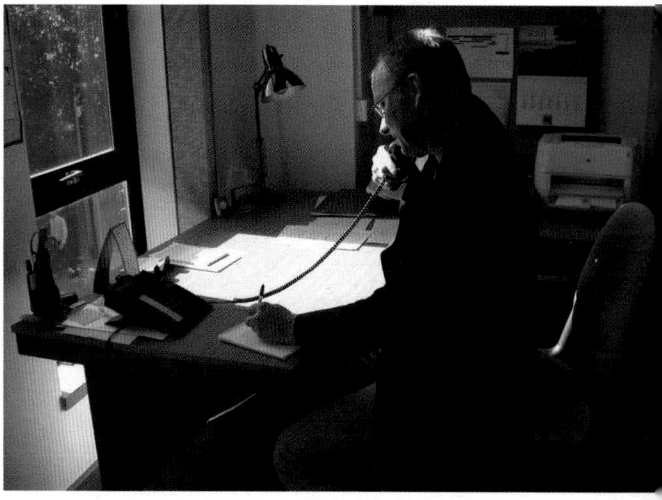

3 Language focus

Listen again and complete the voicemail messages.

1

Hi, Bob. Roger .... I've looked at the designs and I think I'm ready to decide. Can you come to my office tomorrow to discuss them? .... me .... 8993. Bye.

2

Hello. This .... Lena Sampson from Emily Plessey of Net Solutions, telephone 337 8021. I've emailed the proposal you asked for. .... later this week when you've had a chance to look at it. I hope that's OK. Goodbye.

3

Hello Jamie, ... Marlies. How are you? I haven't heard from you about the results of the survey. Can you .... 5536? The sales team is anxious to get the data. Thanks. Bye.

LANGUAGE FILE 2 >> PAGE 98

4 Communication activity

STUDENT A: **Look at the information on page 76.**
STUDENT B: **Look at the information below.**

Situation 1

Leave a voicemail message for Kate Delgado at your Head Office. You know her well.
You want a new price list for printing colour brochures.
Ask about the date for the printing of the new catalogue.

Situation 2

Imagine you are Barry Chapman and you are listening to your voicemail messages. Write down the message that Student A leaves. Then check with him/her that your message is correct.

UNIT 8 Appointments

UNIT GOALS • making appointments • changing appointments

TALKING POINT

Look at these ways of organizing a schedule.
Which do you think is the best/worst? Why?
Which do you use? Why?

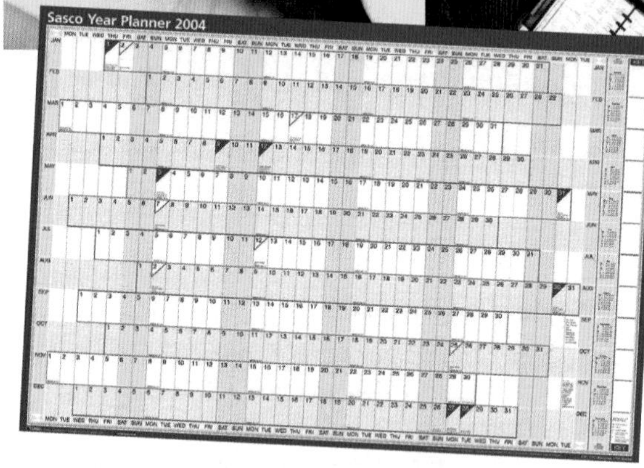

PART A Making an appointment

1 Listening

a Listen to Jenny Young calling Tara Luckman to make an appointment. Answer the questions.

1 When is Jenny free?

2 When is Tara free?

3 When do they decide to meet?

b Put the verbs in brackets into the correct form to complete the things that Jenny and Tara said. Then listen and check.

1

JENNY: I'm free all day Wednesday.

TARA: Sorry, Jenny, I .... (interview) all day Wednesday ... but I'm free all day Thursday.

2

JENNY: Let me see ... I've got plans but I can cancel ... and I .... (visit) another client in the morning so I could come straight to you in the afternoon. Is two o'clock OK?

LANGUAGE FILE 1 >> PAGE 99

2 Language focus

a The table below shows things that Jenny and Tara said in 1 Listening. Choose the best title (a, b or c) for each column in the table.

a Saying that you are available

b Saying that you are not available

c Making a suggestion

1	2	3 ....
Can I come and see you this week? What about Friday? Is two o'clock OK?	I'm free all day Wednesday. I've got nothing in the afternoon. I can cancel. Two o'clock's fine.	Sorry, I'm interviewing all day Wednesday. I'm tied up Thursday morning. I have another appointment on Thursday afternoon. I'm out in the morning.

b Practise in pairs. One student makes a suggestion. The other student agrees, or says he/she is busy and suggests another time.

Example

A: *Can we meet on Tuesday?*

B: *I'm tied up on Tuesday. What about Wednesday?*

LANGUAGE FILE 2 >> **PAGE 99**

3 Communication activity

STUDENT A: **Look at the information on page 79.**
STUDENT B: **Look at the information below.**

You are Sam Beattie, a salesperson for Smooth, a company which supplies soft drinks dispensers for bars. Call Student A, Kim Wesley, the Catering Manager at the Sunrise Hotel.

Look at your schedule (below). Try to make an appointment to show Student A your new improved drinks dispenser.

Mon 13	10.00–12.00 weekly sales meeting
Tue 14	2.00 visit Mary Judd, Pizza Palace
Wed 15	4.00 travel to conference
Thu 16	annual sales conference (all day)
Fri 17	annual sales conference (all day)

4 Culture Focus

In your company/country, what happens if you change an appointment, forget an appointment or arrive late?

PART B Changing an appointment

1 Vocabulary

Match the sentences 1–7 to the explanations a–g.

1 My luggage is missing.	a The train isn't going.
2 The train is delayed.	b We can't move because there are so many cars.
3 The train's cancelled.	c I don't know which way to go.
4 We're stuck in traffic.	d The meeting will now happen at a later time.
5 I'm lost.	e I'm not as early as I need to be.
6 I'm running late.	f The train is late.
7 The meeting was postponed.	g My bags have gone to the wrong place.

VOCABULARY FILE >> **PAGE 101**

2 Listening

a Look at the pictures. Sophie Mueller has an appointment with Frank Cho this afternoon. She planned to travel on flight AI105. With a partner, discuss what you think she says when she calls him.

b Listen to the call and decide if these statements are true (T) or false (F).

1 They cancelled the appointment.

2 They rescheduled the appointment.

3 They're going to meet tomorrow afternoon.

4 They're going to meet tomorrow morning.

c Use the correct form of the verbs in brackets to complete these things that Sophie said. Then listen and check.

1 I'm afraid my flight has been delayed. I'm sorry, but I'm .... (make) it to Seoul in time for our appointment.

2 They say two hours, but most of the flights are delayed. I think it's .... (be) longer than that.

LANGUAGE FILE 3 >> **PAGE 100**

3 Language focus

a Work in pairs. Look at the examples below from 2 Listening. **Use the prompts in the table to make complete sentences about the other situations.**

Problem	Apology and result	Suggestion
flight / delayed *I'm afraid my flight has been delayed.*	not make / Seoul / appointment *I'm sorry, but I'm not going to make it to Seoul in time for our appointment.*	time / meet / morning? *Do you have time to meet me in the morning?*
taxi / traffic	late	put back an hour?
train / cancelled	not make it	reschedule?
lost	a little late	wait for me / start without me?

b Practise in pairs. Take turns to phone each other, explain your problem, apologize and make a suggestion.

LANGUAGE FILE 4 >> PAGE 100

4 Communication activity

STUDENT A: **Look at the information on page 80.**
STUDENT B: **Look at the information below.**

Situation 1

You have an appointment with Student A in Warsaw. Your flight has been delayed. Call Student A, apologize and try to reschedule the appointment. Here is your schedule.

Wednesday 23
a.m. 10.05 fly to Warsaw BA1848
p.m. 2.00 meet Student A

Thursday 24
a.m.
p.m. 3.50 fly to Prague BA1596

Situation 2

Student A will call you. Try to solve any problems and reschedule your appointment if necessary. Here is your schedule.

Mon 19
9.00 report to boss
11.00
2.00 meet Student A, my office
3.00
5.00
5.30 sales meeting
7.00

UNIT

9 Meetings

UNIT GOALS • organizing meetings • taking part in meetings

TALKING POINT

What is the purpose of meetings?
What are the advantages and disadvantages of meetings?

PART A Organizing meetings

1 Vocabulary

Work in pairs. Look at this list of things you need to do when you organize a meeting. Number them in the order in which you should do them.

To do :

☐	a circulate the agenda
☐	b set a date and time
☐	c notify the participants
1	d send out the minutes of the last meeting
☐	e book a room
☐	f prepare the agenda
☐	g check people's availability

VOCABULARY FILE >> PAGE 103

2 Reading

a **Martin is checking people's availability for a meeting. Read his email and extracts from the four replies opposite, and complete his chart. Tick (✓) where people are available, put a cross (✗) where they are not available, and a question mark (?) where they are not sure.**

	Steve	Tina	Anna	Kevin
Tue 28				
Wed 29				
Mon 3				
Tue 4				
Wed 5				
Thu 6				
Fri 7				
Mon 10				

Dear All
[a] We would like to have a one-day meeting to look at our advertising budget for next year and start planning our advertising. [b] Can you let me know your availability for the following dates, please?
28th-29th March
3rd-7th April
10th April

Please reply by 14th March.

Best wishes
Martin

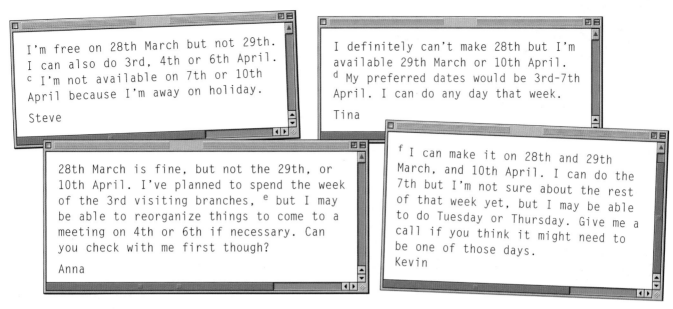

I'm free on 28th March but not 29th. I can also do 3rd, 4th or 6th April. [c] I'm not available on 7th or 10th April because I'm away on holiday.

Steve

I definitely can't make 28th but I'm available 29th March or 10th April. [d] My preferred dates would be 3rd–7th April. I can do any day that week.

Tina

28th March is fine, but not the 29th, or 10th April. I've planned to spend the week of the 3rd visiting branches, [e] but I may be able to reorganize things to come to a meeting on 4th or 6th if necessary. Can you check with me first though?

Anna

[f] I can make it on 28th and 29th March, and 10th April. I can do the 7th but I'm not sure about the rest of that week yet, but I may be able to do Tuesday or Thursday. Give me a call if you think it might need to be one of those days.

Kevin

b Which do you think would be the best days to try and have the meeting?

3 Listening

Listen to Martin speaking to Anna and Kevin on the phone and complete his email with the day, date and time.

Dear All

Thanks for giving me your availability so promptly. [g] The advertising meeting will take place on ...., ..., ... a.m.–5.00 p.m., in Room 306 on the 3rd floor. There will be coffee, lunch and tea.

I will send out the agenda next week.

Regards

Martin

4 Language focus

Match these headings to the phrases a–g in the emails in 2 Reading **and** 3 Listening**.**

1 Saying when you are available
2 Confirming the details of the meeting
3 Saying when you are not available
4 Asking when people are available
5 Explaining the purpose of the meeting
6 Giving preferences
7 Saying when you may be available

LANGUAGE FILE 1 >> PAGE 102

5 Communication activity

a Work in groups of four. You need to organize a half-day meeting for next week, Monday 3rd to Friday 7th September, with the other students in your group.

STUDENT A: **Look at the information on page 79.**
STUDENT B: **Look at the information on page 80.**
STUDENT C: **Look at the information on page 82.**
STUDENT D: **Look at the information on page 81.**

b Read the emails from the others in your group, and note possible times for a meeting. Discuss together the day, date and time when you might have the meeting.

c Write an email confirming the details of the meeting.

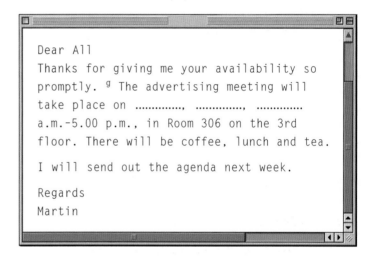

PART B Taking part in meetings

1 Reading

Work in pairs. Read this agenda for a marketing meeting and decide on the best order for the items to be discussed at the meeting.

Marketing team meeting
July 10th, 10.00 a.m.
Room K503

AGENDA		
	Marketing team's activities last month	☐
	Minutes of last meeting	☐
	Apologies for absence	☐
	Ways of getting customer feedback	☐
	Any other business (AOB)	☐
	Marketing team's planned activities for next month	☐

2 Listening

a Work in pairs. Look at these different ways of getting feedback from customers and discuss which one you think is best, and why.

1 send a feedback form with each order ☐
2 send out a questionnaire ☐
3 put a feedback page on the website ☐
4 ask questions face-to-face ☐
5 phone customers ☐
6 offer a free gift in return for feedback ☐

b Listen to part of the marketing meeting about customer feedback. Tick (✓) the ideas above which are mentioned. Which one do they decide on?

c Listen again. What disadvantages are mentioned about the different ways of getting feedback?

3 Language focus

a Match the expressions 1–6 from 2 Listening **to those with a similar meaning a–f.**

1 What do you think?	a Sorry, I missed that.
2 Can I just say something?	b Yes, please do.
3 Sure, go ahead.	c What are your thoughts on this?
4 Sorry to interrupt, but ...	d Let's just recap.
5 Sorry, I didn't quite catch that.	e Sorry to stop you, but ...
6 Shall we just go over what we've said?	f Can I add something?

b Work in groups. Talk about ideas for getting customer feedback, using the phrases above.

LANGUAGE FILE 2 >> **PAGE 103**

4 Communication activity

a Work in groups of four. You all work for a large cosmetics company and are trying to choose a new advertising agency. Your contracting department has found four possible agencies. Read the notes about each one below.

ACE CREATIVES
very creative
experience with big companies
not always flexible
quite expensive

BETTER ADS
new company, very dynamic
not expensive
not much experience
quite a small company

IDEAS NOW
work very fast
good quality advertising
not always reliable
quite expensive

CAMPAIGNERS
very reliable
some very successful advertising
quite expensive
not very creative

b You are going to have a meeting with senior management from different departments of the company, to try and decide which agency to use.

Agenda – senior management meeting
12th May, 10.00–1.00

Apologies for absence
Minutes of last meeting
Sales report
Last year's advertising campaign
Agencies for this year's advertising campaign
AOB
Date of next meeting

STUDENT A: Look at the information on page 79.
STUDENT B: Look at the information on page 80.
STUDENT C: Look at the information on page 82.
STUDENT D: Look at the information on page 81.

c When you have finished your meeting, tell the class what you have decided, and why.

REVIEW 3

Vocabulary 1

Complete the puzzle.

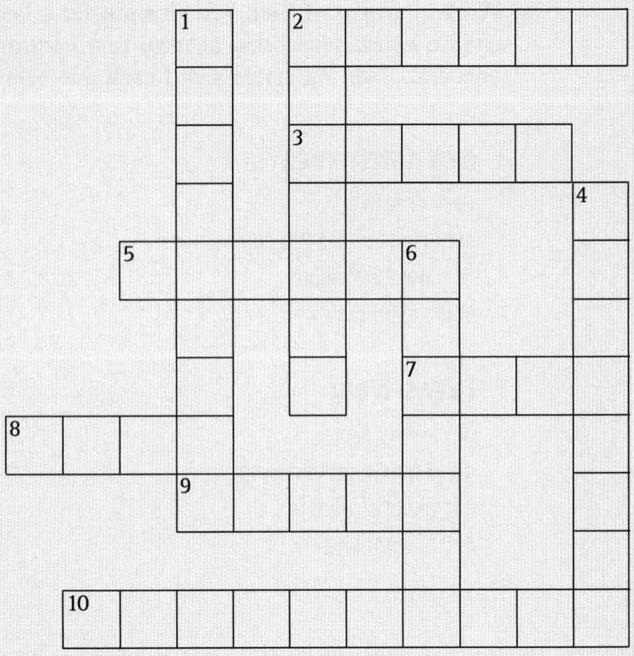

Across

2 Oh no. We've .... our train.

3 I'm afraid I'm .... in traffic.

5 Sorry, I need to go now. I'm running ....

7 I didn't have a map so I got .... on the way to the interview.

8 Sorry I'm .... My car broke down.

9 We regret to announce there will be a two-hour .... because of bad weather.

10 A lot of people are not well. Shall we .... the meeting for next week?

Down

1 The trip was .... because not enough people wanted to go.

2 Some of the documents are .... Has anyone seen them?

4 If the product isn't ready, I think we should .... the launch.

6 I'm afraid my flight's .... because of technical problems.

Language 1

Match the sentences 1–5 to those with a similar meaning a–e.

1 John Craig speaking.
2 He's not available right now.
3 Can I give him a message?
4 Could I visit your office this week?
5 Would you like to leave a message?

a Would it be possible for us to meet this week?
b I'm afraid he's out of the office at the moment.
c This is John Craig.
d Can I leave a message?
e Can I take a message?

Communication 1

With a partner, role play the following situations.

Situation 1

STUDENT A: Call Rita Williams at Sampson Construction. You want to make an appointment to meet her, to show her your company's new construction safety clothing.

STUDENT B: You work for Sampson Construction. Rita Williams is out of the office. Take a message.

Situation 2

STUDENT A: Rita Williams calls you back. Make an appointment to meet her.

STUDENT B: You are Rita Williams. Call Student A back and make an appointment.

Vocabulary 2

Put the words from the box into the best columns below to make phrases used to describe preparations for a meeting.

the minutes	a date and time	people's availability	reception
the participants	a room	the restaurant staff	the agenda
a time limit	individual needs	a finishing time	refreshments

Prepare / Send out / Circulate	Organize/Book	Set/Fix	Notify	Check

Language 2

Match the advice about meetings 1–10 to the expressions a–j.

Before the meeting ...

1 Tell everyone why you are having a meeting.
2 Find out when people can come.
3 Say when you can come.
4 Say when you can't come.
5 Confirm the details of the meeting.

At the meeting ...

6 Invite other people to speak.
7 Ask others to clarify.
8 Ask if you can speak.
9 Review what people have said.
10 Discuss who is going to do things.

a Sorry, I didn't quite catch that. What did you say?
b The meeting will be on Wed 10th April, from 9.30 to 12.30, in Room G3.
c We would like to have a meeting to discuss the new product brochure.
d I can make it on Thursday 14th June.
e So, first of all, we need to decide who's going to prepare the survey.
f I can't do Monday or Tuesday.
g Can I just add something?
h What are your thoughts on this?
i Can you tell me if you are available on Wednesday or Thursday next week?
j Shall we just go over what we've said so far?

Communication 2

Work in groups. Your company wants to write a document on 'best practice' for using the telephone. Make a list of things to talk about. Now have a meeting to discuss exactly what the document should say.

Decide on a standard telephone greeting.
Decide on a standard procedure for taking messages.

UNIT

10 Negotiating

UNIT GOALS • negotiating with colleagues • negotiating with other companies

TALKING POINT

What kind of things do you need to negotiate ...
... with colleagues?
... with other companies?
Is it more difficult to negotiate with colleagues, or with other companies?

PART A Negotiating with colleagues

1 Brainstorming

Work in pairs. Which of these things do you think are most important for a successful meeting with a possible new client? Can you think of anything else which is not on this list?

1	the programme for the day	☐	6	price lists	☐
2	an agenda for the meeting	☐	7	a presentation	☐
3	a staff list	☐	8	a tour of the office/factory	☐
4	business cards	☐	9	lunch	☐
5	product brochures	☐	10	tea and coffee	☐

2 Listening

a Clive and Gemma are preparing for a meeting with three representatives from a company which may become a new client. Listen to their conversation, and tick (✓) the things in 1 Brainstorming which they mention.

b Complete the sentences with gaps from Clive and Gemma's conversation.

Ask someone to do something

1 Can you send those out now?
2 Could you do that/it?
3 Do you .... take over for production times and delivery schedules?
4 .... to do that/it?

Accepting a task

5 ...., no problem.
6 Yes, that's ....

Offering to do something

7 Do .... send the brochures?
8 .... give the presentation.
9 I'll do that.

Rejecting a task

10 I'd .... not, if possible.
11 I'd .... not to talk about processes, if that's OK.
12 I might not have time to do that.

c Listen again. Look at the list of tasks and write down who agrees to do which task. Write G (for Gemma) or C (for Clive).

1	.... send brochures	5	.... discuss product processes
2	.... get price lists	6	.... discuss delivery schedules
3	.... give presentation	7	.... deal with lunch arrangements
4	.... introductions	8	.... arrange factory tour

LANGUAGE FILE 1 >> PAGE 104

3 Language focus

a Look at these sentences with *if* from 2 Listening.

1 If you welcome them and introduce everyone at the start, I'll give the presentation.

2 I'll talk about the product range and production times **if** you discuss delivery schedules.

b Match the sentence halves to make complete sentences with *if*.

1	If you go and meet Carla at reception,	a	if I prepare it?
2	We'll leave the equipment in the room	b	he'll bring it to the meeting room.
3	If I find out what kind of food everyone likes,	c	if you don't have time for them.
4	I'll do those minutes tomorrow	d	will you organize lunch?
5	If you tell Peter exactly what equipment you need,	e	if you put it away at the end.
6	Will you send out the agenda	f	I'll check that the room is ready for her.

LANGUAGE FILE 2 >> PAGE 105

4 Communication activity

Your company is going to launch a new product next month.
You have to organize a special launch event.

a Look at the list of jobs that have to be done. Think about which you would like to do, and why.

- organize publicity
- organize food and drink
- choose a location
- organize entertainment
- choose a famous person to attend and promote the product
- hire temporary staff
- plan the schedule for the event
- prepare a speech to give

b Work in pairs. Negotiate who is going to do each job and why.

5 Reporting

What did you decide? Who is going to do each task, and why?

PART B Business negotiations

1 Vocabulary

a Match the adverts 1–6 to the sentences a–f.

1 **10% discount**

2 60 days credit terms

3 free service contract

4 **extended warranty**

5 *fast delivery*

6 no shipping costs

a We can bring it to you in two days.

b We will repair the product free.

c We will reduce the price.

d You don't have to pay for 60 days.

e You don't pay anything for us to send it to you.

f We will repair the product free after the guarantee ends.

b Work in pairs. Discuss which of the six things above you would find most attractive, as a customer.

VOCABULARY FILE >> PAGE 106

2 Language focus

a Look at these typical stages in a negotiation:

A makes a request.	We'd like you to deliver the goods next week.
B refuses, and makes a counter suggestion.	We're sorry, but we need two weeks to prepare the order.
A agrees but adds a condition.	That's OK if you can offer free delivery.
B agrees.	That's fine.
OR	
B doesn't agree immediately.	I'll have to think about it and get back to you.

b Use the prompts to have negotiations.

Example

A: finish the project next week — *We'd like you to finish the project next week.*

B: not possible – need three weeks — *We're sorry, but we need three weeks to finish it.*

A: OK if 3% discount — *That's OK if you can give us a 3% discount.*

B: not sure — *I'll have to check with my manager and call you back.*

1 A: want delivery next month
B: no problem

2 A: want 10% discount
B: can give 5%
A: OK if 90-day terms
B: OK

3 A: want one-year free service contract
B: can give six months
A: OK if discount
B: not sure

LANGUAGE FILE 3 >> PAGE 106

3 Listening

a **Listen to extracts from four different negotiations and complete the table.**

	Request	Counter suggestion	Conditions
1			
2			
3			
4			

b **Work in pairs. Have negotiations using the information in the table.**

4 Communication activity

STUDENT A: **Look at the information on page 81.**
STUDENT B: **Look at the information below.**

Situation 1

You are a sales representative for Comlink Ltd. You sell computers. Student A is a customer.

- You usually offer 5% discount on PCs and 7.5% discount on monitors; for a large order you sometimes offer 10% on PCs and monitors.
- You usually deliver in two weeks, but you can deliver more quickly if necessary.
- You offer a free one-year service contract, which you can extend to two years for a small fee.

Enter into a negotiation with Student A. You don't want to lose the customer but you need to make the best possible deal. Make notes of your deal.

Situation 2

Your company wants to buy ten vans. Student A works for Delta Motors Ltd.

This is what you want:

- 15% discount if possible, but you can accept less if the company offers you something else.
- The vans must be repainted in your company colours. This normally costs about 1,000 a van, but you want to pay less than that.
- Delivery next month – this is very important for you.

Enter into a negotiation with Student A. You want to get the best possible deal.
Make notes of your deal.

5 Writing

Write an email to the customer who you negotiated with in 4 Communication activity, **confirming the details.**

Following our recent telephone conversation, I am writing to confirm what we discussed.

You would like to order …

For an order of this size, we can offer a discount of .... %, and ....

We can deliver this order …

Please confirm in writing within 30 days.

UNIT

11 Money

UNIT GOALS • exchanging money and using numbers • payment methods

TALKING POINT

What is the currency in your country?
What other currencies have you used?
Do you think every country should use the same currency?
What different ways are there to pay for goods and services?

PART A Exchanging money

1 Vocabulary

How many different currencies do you know? Match the currencies to these places. Some currencies go with more than one place.

1 dollar	2 euro	3 franc	4 krona	5 lira
6 peso	7 pound	8 rand	9 rouble	10 yen

Australia ....
Argentina ....
Europe ....
Japan ....
Mexico ....
Russia ....
South Africa ....
Switzerland ....
Sweden ....
Turkey ....
UK ....
USA ....

VOCABULARY FILE 1 >> PAGE 109

2 Language focus

Work in pairs. Can you say the amounts of money in these news stories?

Example
€13,398,122 *thirteen million, three hundred and ninety-eight thousand, one hundred and twenty-two euros*

1 The Geneva-based company made a profit of SFr 913,703 last year.

2 **Baugur believes that Hamleys toy store is worth $94,450,000.**

3 Greene King's sales for the year stand at £535,600,000.

4 The car, which costs €86,975, has the very latest safety and performance technology.

5 **At ¥2,165, the new computer is a bargain for Japanese enthusiasts.**

6 ***Her annual salary is Skr 593,000 (€65,056).***

Compare with another pair.

LANGUAGE FILE 1 >> PAGE 107

3 Listening

a Listen to three conversations in which people are exchanging money. Complete the first two columns in the table.

	Currency → Currency	Amount to change	Exchange rate	Amount received
1				
2				
3				

b Listen again and complete the last two columns in the table.

c Who says each of these things from the listening – the customer or the bank clerk?

1 The exchange rate is 1.35 to the dollar.
2 Can I change euros to South African rand, please?
3 You'll receive 5,940 rand.
4 What's the exchange rate?
5 I'd like to change 750 euros, please.
6 75 yen to the dollar.
7 I'd like to buy Japanese yen, please, with Australian dollars.
8 I'll change 400 dollars, please.
9 I'd like to change US dollars to Swiss francs, please.
10 It's eight rand to the euro at the moment.

LANGUAGE FILE 2 >> PAGE 108

4 Communication activity

STUDENT A: **Look at the information on page 82.**
STUDENT B: **Look at the information below.**

Situation 1
You are a customer at a bank in Rome. Student A is a bank clerk. Ask to change €1,000 into these currencies:

- Russian roubles
- Japanese yen
- Australian dollars

Make a note of how much you get for each transaction.

Situation 2
You are a bank clerk in Athens. Student A is a customer. Use the information below to answer Student A's questions.

Exchange rates	
€1 = R8 (South African rand)	€1,000 = R8,000 (South African rand)
€1 = US$1.1	€1,000 = US$1,100
€1 = SFr1.5	€1,000 = SFr1,500

PART B Payment methods

1 Vocabulary

a Complete the labels for the front and back of a credit card using the words in the box.

security number card number
expiry date cardholder signature

1 ....

2 ....

3 ....

4 ....

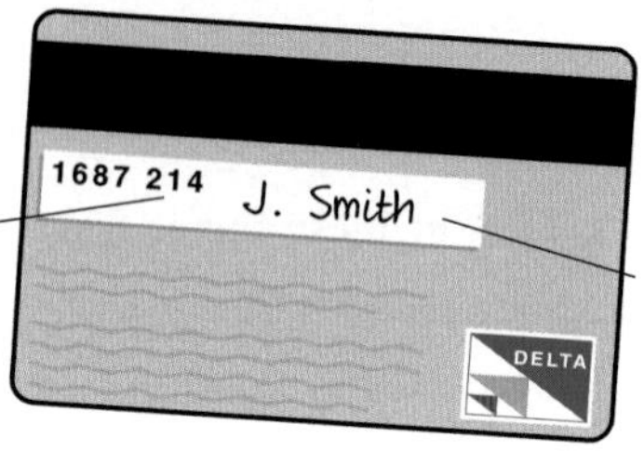

5 ....

2 Listening

a When making a payment, what four pieces information do the customer and the supplier need to give?

1 For a credit card transaction, the customer needs to give:

card number ....

....

2 For a bank transfer, the supplier needs to give:

....

....

b Listen to two conversations between customers and suppliers and check your answers.

VOCABULARY FILE 2 >> PAGE 109

3 Language focus

a Complete the questions in the conversations from 2 Listening**.**

1
Can I have ...., please?
Yes, it's 4929 1234 5678 9012.
And the .... date?
That's, er, 09/08.
And .... in your name?
Yes, D Buckley, that's right.
And can .... the security number?

2
What's the ....?
Connect Trading Limited.
What's .... code?
44-08-36.
And .... number?
98765432.
Could I have .... of your bank, too?
Sure. It's ABC Commercial Bank, Marstown Branch. That's at 48, High Street, Marstown, MT8 9PP.

b Listen again and check.

LANGUAGE FILE 3 >> PAGE 108

4 Communication activity

STUDENT A: Look at the information on page 84.
STUDENT B: Look at the information below.

Situation 1
You are a customer service agent taking orders by phone. Student A is a customer.
Answer Student A's questions using the information below.

Bank transfer

Account name:	Swiftplan
Account number:	88531044
Sort code:	56-21-70
Bank:	Hanson Bank, Chorley branch
Bank address:	10A Middle Road, Chorley

Situation 2
You are a customer service agent taking telephone orders by phone. Student A is a customer.
Ask Student A questions so that you can complete the form below.

Credit card transaction

Card type ....

Card number ....

Expiry date ....

Cardholder ....

Security number ....

5 Culture focus

Discuss these questions in small groups.

1 Which of these methods of payment have you or your company used?

- cash
- cheque
- travellers' cheques
- credit card
- bank transfer
- regular direct debit (e.g. monthly, quarterly, or annual)
- other, for example ....

2 When is each method most useful?

Example cash – *buying drinks/snacks in a café*

3 What are the advantages and disadvantages of each method?

Example *Cash is quick and convenient, but it's easy to lose or have stolen.*

UNIT

12 Marketing

UNIT GOALS • discussing marketing methods • talking about websites

TALKING POINT

What is marketing?
What are the different forms of marketing?
Do you think the Internet is useful for marketing?
What do you most like and dislike about the Internet?

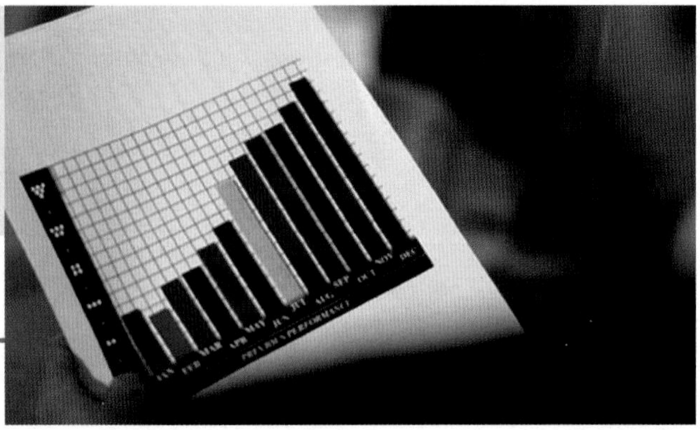

PART A Ways of marketing

1 Vocabulary

Match the different forms of marketing 1–6 to the advantages and disadvantages a–f.

1 direct mail
2 telemarketing
3 print advertising
4 billboards
5 TV advertising
6 sponsorship

a It can be very expensive, but it **reaches a wide audience.**

b You talk directly to **potential customers** and can **get good results**, but many customers don't like being phoned like this.

c If it's a popular sport, you can **get good coverage**. Smaller events don't **reach** so many people though.

d It's easy to do and **cost-effective**, but many people call it 'junk mail' and throw it away without reading it.

e This is a fairly cheap way to **get good exposure**. You need to make sure you have a **good location**, though.

f You can **target your market** well if you choose the right paper or magazine. You need quite a big **budget**, though.

VOCABULARY FILE 1 >> PAGE 111

2 Listening

a Listen to the Marketing Manager of a cosmetics company talking about the marketing activities of his company. Tick (✓) the activities the company uses.

TV advertising ☐ print advertising ☐ billboards ☐
direct mail ☐ telemarketing ☐ sponsorship ☐

b What reasons does he give for doing or not doing each activity? Listen again and check.

3 Language focus

Complete the things the Marketing Manager said in 2 Listening. Then listen again and check.

1 We would like .... TV advertising.
2 I'm sure a lot of people enjoy .... the adverts.
3 They can't avoid .... our adverts.
4 I think we need .... our billboard advertising.
5 Last year we decided .... direct mail.
6 We're planning .... our whole marketing strategy.

LANGUAGE FILE >> PAGE 110

4 Communication activity

STUDENT A: **Look at the information on page 84.**
STUDENT B: **Look at the information below.**

Situation 1
Student A's company is marketing a new mobile phone. Think of some questions you could ask Student A about his/her marketing plans. Use these examples and ideas to help you.

- What's the product?
- What's the market?
- What ... planning ... do?
- What ... need ... ?
- What / decide ... ?
- What / avoid ... ?
- ... ?

Ask Student A about his/her marketing plans and make notes.

Situation 2
Your company is marketing a new soft drink. Read the information below.

Zest fruit drink
Market: children aged 7–12
Marketing activity:

- TV advertisements between children's programmes – reach a lot of people.
- Colour advertisements in children's comics and magazines – reach the right market.
- Free drink promotion outside shops – children can try the new drink.
- Not sponsorship – children of this age don't watch much sport on TV, and research shows they don't pay attention to the advertising there.

Think about how to describe your marketing. Use these examples and ideas to help you.

- The product is a fruit drink.
- The market is children ...
- We're (not) planning to ...
- We've decided (not) to ...
- We're going to avoid ...
- We ...

Answer Student A's questions about your marketing.

5 Exploring

a Work in pairs to plan a marketing campaign.

You are responsible for planning the marketing activity for a new teenage magazine. It is aimed at 14–16-year-olds and will contain articles on music, fashion, films and computer games.

Discuss how you will market the magazine. You have a limited budget, so you can only choose up to three ways of marketing. Decide which ways you will and won't use, and why. Give details. (For example, if you want to sponsor an event, what should it be? Why?)

b Explain your choice to another pair. Explain why you won't use other ways of marketing.

PART B Talking about websites

1 Vocabulary

Complete the comments about websites below, using the words in the box.

colours	drop-down	icons	layout	links
menu	scroll	search	slow	writing

1 It's really .... I have to wait ages for each page to appear on the screen.

2 The .... was difficult to read because it was so small.

3 I think the .... are excellent. The green and blue look very attractive together.

4 I found the .... very confusing. I didn't know which part of the page to go to.

5 If you want more information about the subject, there are a lot of useful .... to other websites.

6 There's always a .... on the left, so you can easily choose a different page to go to.

7 There were too many .... menus, where you have to click on an arrow then a list appears for you to choose from.

8 The page is very long, so you have to .... down a long way to find the information you need.

9 There's a very good .... facility to help you find what you want.

10 I found it hard to click on the .... because they were so small.

VOCABULARY FILE 2 >> PAGE 111

2 Brainstorming

Work in pairs. Look at these headings for pages on a website. What do you expect to find on each page?

Home | About us | Contact us | Products/Services | Newsletter | Competition

3 Reading

Read the text about what makes a good website. Match each point to one of the page headings.

About us | Contact us | Products/Services | Newsletter | Competition

1 A website must give clear opportunities for visitors to get in touch with you easily and quickly.
2 You should encourage people who visit your website to subscribe to receive regular information from the company. This is a good way of getting their contact details.
3 It's good to have a description of your company to give confidence to new customers.
4 You should have a way of getting visitors to return frequently to your site. Many sites have a special promotion or quiz which changes regularly.
5 Provide clear links to what your company has to offer. This can range from general information on what's available to full online purchasing or signing up for more information.

4 Exploring

a Work in pairs. Look at this page from a website. Discuss whether this is a well-designed website or not. Which features do you particularly like? Which would you like to change? Why?

b Work with another pair. Redesign the web page.

REVIEW 4

Vocabulary 1

Find ten currency words in this wordsearch. There are five across and five down.

R	O	L	L	A	R	A	N	F	C	A
O	A	N	S	H	I	L	L	P	O	S
U	X	O	T	B	F	K	I	F	R	E
B	S	S	Y	E	G	R	R	T	Y	U
L	D	M	P	E	S	O	T	U	R	J
E	U	R	O	P	R	N	S	V	W	N
E	R	O	U	B	T	A	Q	U	I	R
S	Y	E	N	T	U	B	L	R	P	M
N	E	X	D	O	L	L	A	R	O	O
O	V	E	S	P	G	I	F	A	U	N
R	K	R	O	N	F	R	A	N	C	T
N	S	C	V	A	L	A	N	D	J	H

Language 1

Write responses to the statements below. Use the prompts to help you.

1 We'd like a 20% discount. (Agree – but customer must order more than 100 units.)

That's fine, but we would like you to order more than 100 units.

2 We'll repeat our order if you give us a 10% discount. (Agree.)

3 We want our company logo on the product. (Refuse – not company policy.)

4 We'd like six months' credit. (Think about it.)

5 We'd like delivery in two weeks. (Agree – if customer pays for air freight.)

Communication 1

a Look at this list of tasks to do in an office. Decide which ones you would prefer to do, and why.

Check the coffee machine.
Check emails from the website.
Fill the photocopier with paper.
Check for any overnight incoming faxes.
Check the paper in the fax machine.
Check the paper in all the printers.
Prepare the room for today's department meeting.
Go to the department meeting and take the minutes.
Answer the phones while everyone else is at the department meeting.
Deal with visitors/calls for the office manager.

b Work in pairs. Negotiate who is going to do each task, and why.

Vocabulary 2

Work in pairs. Discuss these different ways of marketing a product and decide which would work well, and not so well, for the industry you work in or would like to work in. Use some of the phrases below to give your reasons.

billboards	direct mail	Internet marketing	
print advertising	sponsorship	telemarketing	TV advertising

potential customers	reach a wide audience	get good coverage
get good exposure	good location	budget
target your market	cost-effective	get good results

Language 2

Work in pairs. Below is a telephone conversation between a travel agent and a customer. Put the conversation in the correct order.

a And the expiry date, please? ☐
b Could I pay for the ticket now, please? *1*
c 09/07. ☐
d Certainly. How would you like to pay? ☐
e Thank you. We'll drop the ticket off to your office today. ☐
f Visa, OK. And the number? ☐
g By credit card. ☐
h OK. What type of card is it? ☐
i 1234 5678 098 536. ☐
j It's a Visa card. ☐

Communication 2

Think of three items you own (e.g. bicycle, car, house, computer, mobile phone). Decide how much you would sell each one for, and what the conditions might be (e.g. credit terms, cost of delivery, delivery time).

Walk around the class. Try to sell your items to your classmates. Negotiate the best deal you can.

UNIT

13 Networking

UNIT GOALS • meeting people and making contacts • following up

TALKING POINT

Which of these are good places to meet people from other companies socially?

- parties
- restaurants
- sports clubs
- conferences
- professional organizations

What are the advantages of meeting people from other companies socially?
How much do you, or would you, do it?

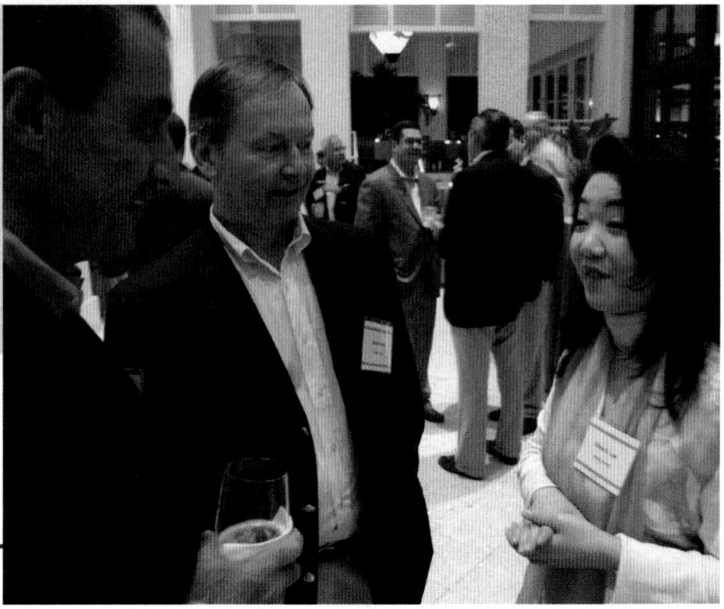

PART A Meeting people

1 Culture focus

a Work in pairs and answer the questions.

1 What is networking?
  a using the Internet at work
  b making computers
  c meeting business people socially
2 Why network?
  a to earn a salary
  b to make useful business contacts
  c to find out important information
3 What is 'personal networking'?
  a making contacts through friends and family
  b making special computers for individuals
  c visiting websites not related to work

b Read the article and check your answers.

c Discuss these questions.

1 Do you agree with everything the article says?
2 Can you think of any disadvantages to networking?
3 Is networking popular in your country?
4 How do you feel if someone is more successful than you because of their contacts?

It's not what you know, it's who you know ...

WHAT IS NETWORKING?

Networking is the process of meeting other business people in social situations, to exchange information and ideas, and make useful contacts. By networking, through a 'web' of connections, you build up relationships with many people and develop trust and communication with them.

WHY NETWORK?

Networking could help you find your first job or change to a better one, receive personal advice, develop as an employee, find new clients or generate new business opportunities. And it is a two-way process; by networking you make opportunities for others and help them achieve their goals, and in return, they will support you. The individual who has the right answer for you or knows the right people might be just one contact away from you. Networking is an important, invaluable, and essential activity that everyone should practise.

PERSONAL NETWORKING

It is important to take advantage of personal contacts, too. Through connections with friends, family, and acquaintances, trustworthy relationships develop that can generate information, advice, support, energy, clients and much more. Next time you have a game of squash with a friend, or go to a party at a relative's house, remember it may be an opportunity to move outside your immediate network and exploit other people's networks, perhaps very different from your own.

2 Listening

Listen to a conversation at a function organized by Doing Business, a networking organization for business people. Answer the questions.

1 What kind of company does George Farley work for?

2 Who does Isaac Bennett work for?

3 Is Isaac's magazine in production at the moment?

4 Why is Isaac at this function?

5 Does Isaac play a lot of squash?

6 Why should Isaac join the squash ladder?

3 Language focus

Complete the sentences from 2 Listening**. Then listen again and check.**

1 Come over here, Isaac. There's .... meet.

2 George, can .... Isaac Bennett? He's a new member. Isaac, ... George Farley.

3 Really? ...., Isaac.

4 There are lots of banking people in the squash ladder. .... join – .... banking people!

5 Excellent. Thanks .... Who .... to about this squash ladder?

6 Ah, there she is. Come on, ...

LANGUAGE FILE 1 >> PAGE 112

4 Communication activity

STUDENT A: **Look at the information on page 83.**
STUDENT B: **Look at the information below.**

Situation 1
You are attending a Doing Business meeting for the first time. You are the Business Development Officer for a company which imports chocolates. You want to meet people who work for department stores. You have just been introduced to Student A. Chat with Student A and see if you can help each other.

Situation 2
You are at a British Chamber of Commerce meeting. You are a restaurant owner. On the other side of the room you can see a customer, Warren McCarthy, who works for a publishing company. You heard that his company will be moving to a new, bigger office soon. You have invited Warren to a private dinner at your restaurant next Thursday evening. Start a conversation with Student A. Find out what he/she does, then offer to introduce Student A to Warren McCarthy.

PART B Following up

1 Reading

a Read this article about how to network. Match the advice 1–8 to the reasons a–h.

EIGHT STEPS TO BETTER NETWORKING

1 Prepare and learn a 30-second description of what you do.

2 Always have some business cards with you.

3 Talk to as many people as possible at social functions.

4 Talk to a mix of people you know and people you haven't met before.

5 Listen carefully to people's introductions, and ask direct questions about them.

6 Keep good records of your contacts, their work and interests.

7 Help contacts with their problems.

8 Always follow up a meeting with a phone call or email.

a You can find the best person easily when you need help or advice.

b You can introduce yourself quickly and clearly to possible contacts.

c You can maintain old contacts and make new ones.

d This gives people a positive impression and so they are more likely to help you in future.

e You'll make more contacts.

f You'll find out how someone might be a useful contact.

g People will see you as a problem-solver and will want to help you too.

h You don't know when you might meet a useful business contact.

b Which things in the article do you do or would you do? Why / Why not?

2 Listening

Listen to a conversation a few weeks later between Isaac and George from Part A. Decide if these statements are true (T) or false (F).

1 Isaac has made some contacts since he first met George.

2 Isaac called George to sell some magazines.

3 Isaac suggests a game of squash with George.

4 Isaac wants to introduce George to a department store manager.

3 Language focus

a Complete the sentences from 2 Listening**. Then listen again and check.**

1 This is Isaac Bennett. .... Doing Business a few weeks ago.

2 How are you? How .... ?

3 I made .... playing squash, just as you said ...

4 I .... the favour. I heard from Felicity that you play golf.

5 I'm playing golf .... manages a department store and I thought .... her.

6 That's .... When are you playing?

b Practise the conversation between Isaac and George.

LANGUAGE FILE 2 >> PAGE 112

4 Communication activity

Work in pairs and practise this conversation.

Last week Student B (a financial services provider) was introduced to a contact by Student A (an import agent for food products). The contact was very useful and as a result Student B has gained several new customers. Student B calls Student A to say thank you and return the favour by introducing him/her to a fresh-food wholesaler.

Student A	**Student B**
Answer the phone. →	
	Say who you are.
← Say hello and ask about Student B's business. →	
	Explain how things are going. Thank Student A for the contact.
← Respond. →	
	Explain that you are meeting a fresh-food wholesaler that you know. Offer to introduce Student A to him/her.
← Respond. →	
	Close the conversation.
← Close the conversation.	

5 Writing

Soon after meeting George at Doing Business, Isaac sent this email thanking George for his help.

To: gfarley@gemsimport.co.uk
From: isaac.bennett@financialreview.com
Subject: Thank you

Dear George
It was good to meet you last week at Doing Business. Thank you very much for introducing me to Felicity Wells. I joined the squash ladder as you suggested and I have already met a few people who are interested in my magazine.
I hope I can return the favour some time.

Regards
Isaac Bennett

With a partner, write the email George sends to Isaac after they play golf, thanking him for the game and for the introduction to Melissa Abdul, the department store manager.

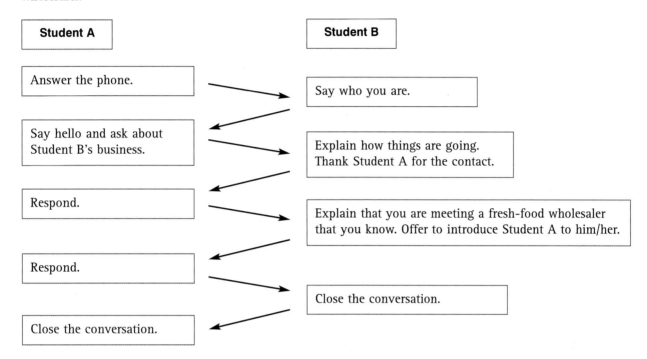

UNIT

14 Trends

UNIT GOALS • talking about changes and trends • describing and predicting performance

TALKING POINT

How has your town/country/company/college changed in recent years?
How do you think it will change in the next few years?
Do you think it is easy to predict what changes will occur?

PART A Recent trends

1 Vocabulary

a Match the percentages 1–8 to the fractions a–h.

1 10%	5 66.6%	a two thirds	e nine tenths
2 20%	6 50%	b a third	f a fifth
3 25%	7 75%	c three quarters	g a quarter
4 33.3%	8 90%	d a tenth	h half

b Work in pairs. Look at the numbers in bold in the newspaper extracts. How could you express them as a fraction? How could you express them as a percentage?

1 We asked 800 people, and **400** of them said they preferred our products.

2 They make 150 different products – **100** in Asia, and **50** in Europe.

3 Because of a bad storm on Monday, only **300** of our employees came to work. **900** of them had to stay at home.

4 1,000,000 people bought a mobile phone last year. **200,000** of them bought one from our company.

5 **1,800** shareholders voted in favour of the changes; only **200** of them voted against.

VOCABULARY FILE >> **PAGE 115**

2 Listening

a Listen to two people from Miranda Beauty talking about their company's products. Match the charts and graphs 1–4 to the products opposite. (2005 is 'now'.)

1

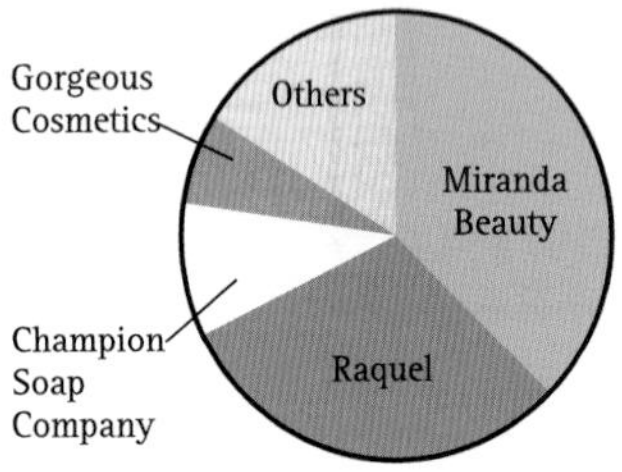

2

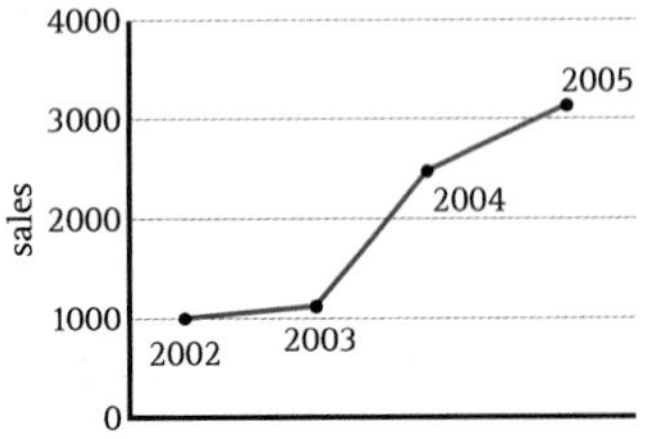

3

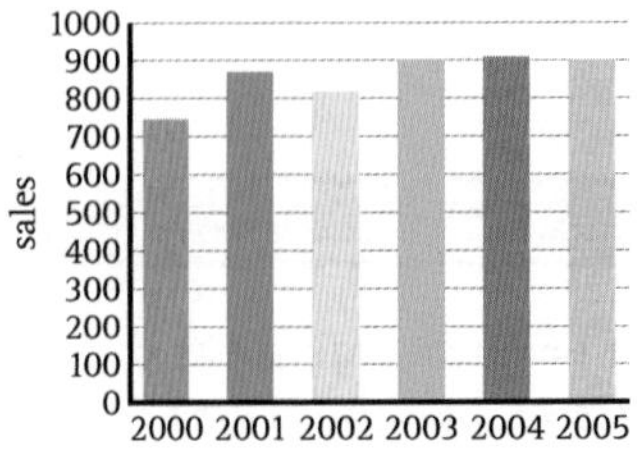

4

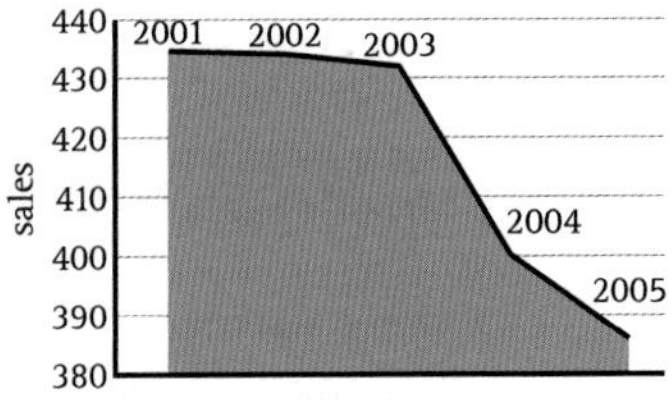

mouthwash

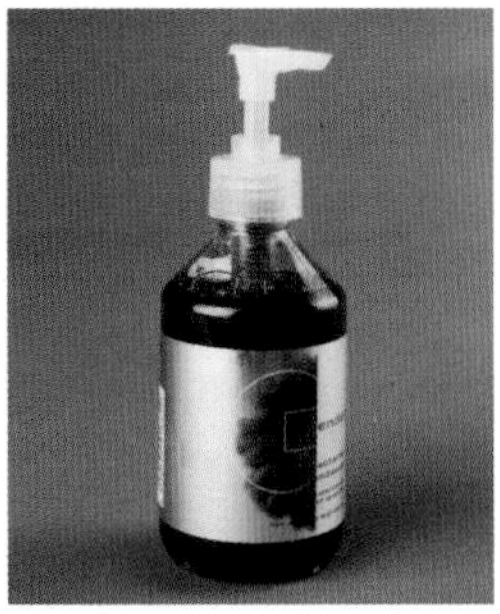

liquid soap

bars of soap

haircare products

3 Language focus

a The words in each of the groups 1–5 have the same meaning. Match the groups to the graphs.

1

go up	a bit
increase	a little
rise	slightly

2

go down	a bit
decrease	a little
fall	slightly

3

stay	the same
remain	steady

4

go up	dramatically
increase	a lot
rise	sharply

5

go down	dramatically
decrease	a lot
fall	sharply

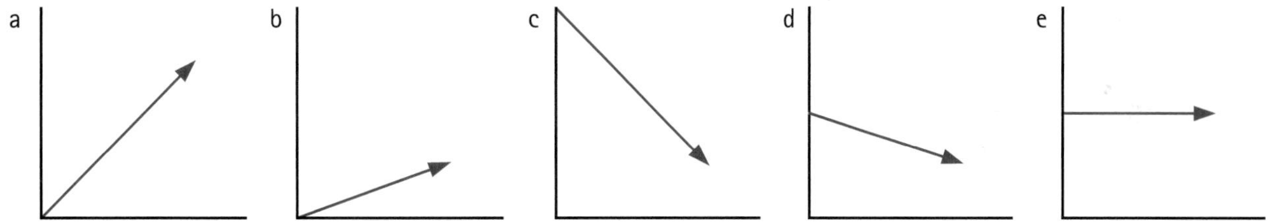

b Listen to the two people from Miranda Beauty again. Complete the things they say below, using words from (a) in the correct form.

1 Sales have .... Just as we predicted.

2 But they .... as .... as last year.

3 Well, no. But they have ....

4 In fact, sales have only .... since 2001.

5 Hmm. What's this one? Sales have .... here.

6 That's not good. They've .... over the last two years.

LANGUAGE FILE 1 >> PAGE 113

4 Communication activity

Work in pairs. You both work for the same company but you each have information about recent sales of different products.

STUDENT A: **Look at the information on page 83.**
STUDENT B: **Look at the information on page 85.**

PART B Predictions

1 Listening

Listen to a Sales Manager talking about his predictions for sales of two products. Complete the two graphs. (2005 is 'now'.)

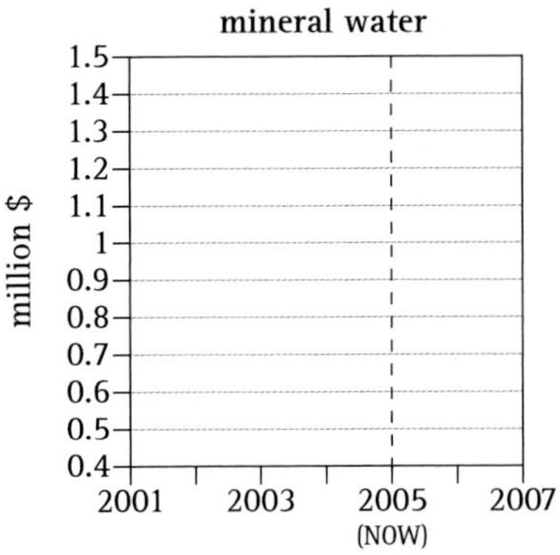

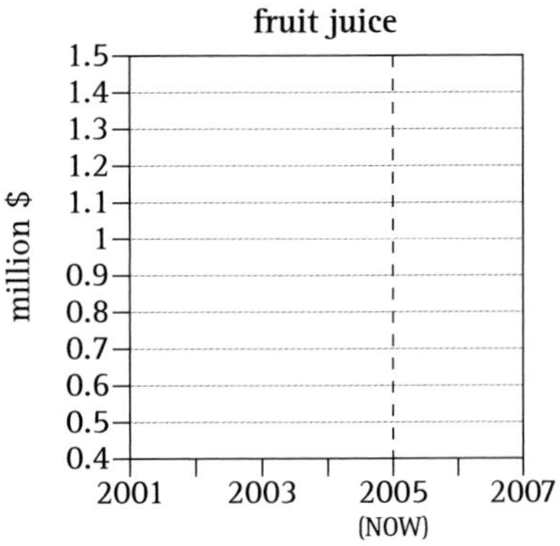

2 Language focus

Complete the things the Sales Manager said in 1 Listening. Then listen again and check.

1 I .... go up again in 2006 and 2007.

2 I don't .... be a big increase.

3 Sales .... go up at the same steady rate of increase.

4 By 2007, I .... achieve sales of about one and a quarter million.

5 I don't think .... any rapid increases.

6 Our .... maintain the current level of sales through 2006 and 2007.

7 In fact, ... sales will increase a little next year.

8 They .... get back to the level of 2001 for quite some time.

LANGUAGE FILE 2 >> PAGE 114

3 Communication activity

With a partner, describe these graphs. (2005 is 'now'.)

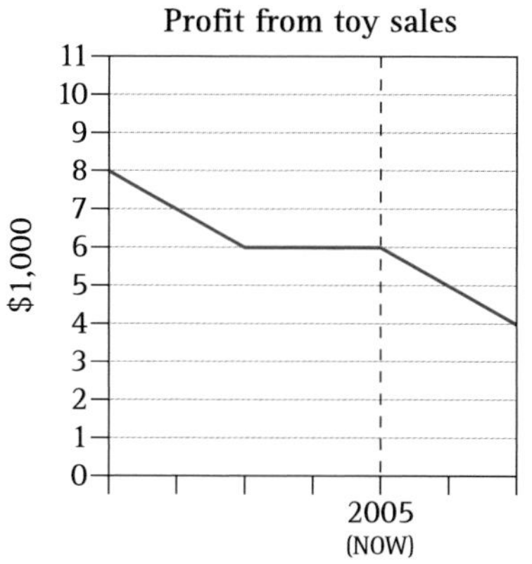

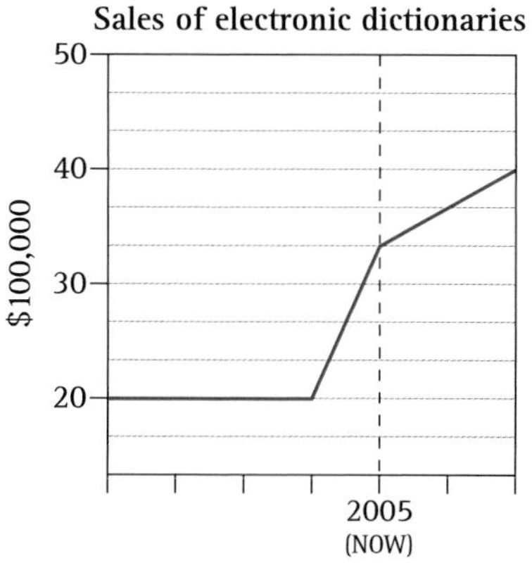

4 Exploring

a Draw lines on the graph to represent your ability in different aspects of English. Choose three or four from listening, speaking, reading, writing, grammar, vocabulary. Use a different colour for each one.

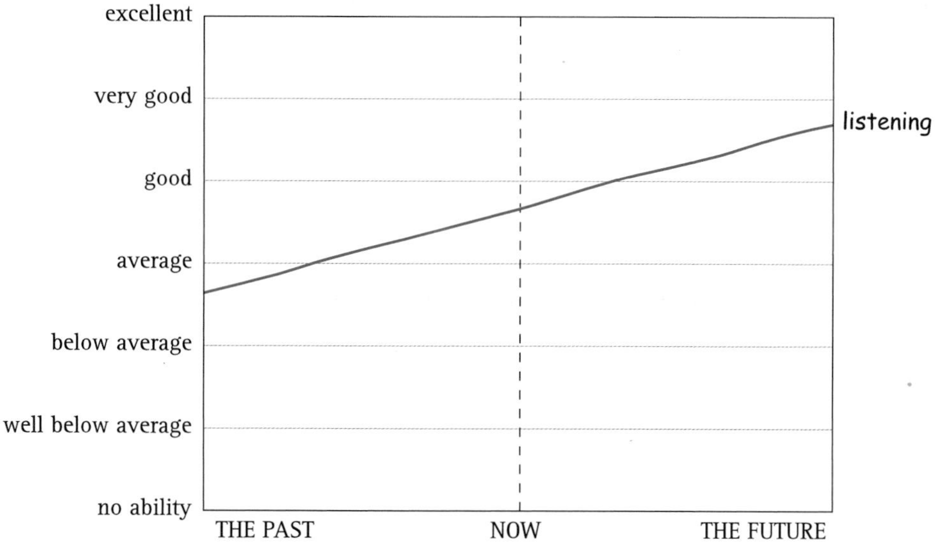

b Work in pairs and discuss your graphs.

UNIT

15 Presenting information

UNIT GOALS • giving a progress report • giving a presentation

TALKING POINT

What is a progress report? What are the advantages of giving a progress report?
What makes a good presentation? What makes a bad one?

PART A Progress reports

1 Listening

a Naomi Taylor's company is building a new website. Listen to the first part of her progress report on the project, and put these four stages in order.

1 reorganizing the customer services department ☐ ....
2 building the website ☐ ....
3 deciding on a website designer ☐ ....
4 planning the website ☐ ....

b Now listen to the next part of Naomi's progress report. Which stages are done and which are not done? Write D or ND next to each one.

2 Language focus

Done:	We've *already* bought new software.	(This has happened before now.)
Not done yet:	We haven't installed it *yet.*	(This hasn't happened up to now.)
In progress:	They are *still* using the old system.	(This is continuing.)

With a partner, complete the sentences using the verbs in brackets and *already, still* or *yet.*

Done

1 Several of you here today ......have already given...... (give) us ideas.
2 We .... (choose) i2i Media to make the website.
3 Several key personnel .... (take) training courses.
4 We .... (buy) new software to help with the day-to-day running of the department.

Not done yet

5 We ......haven't put...... (put) the website online ......yet...... .
6 We .... (not install) it ....
7 They .... (not start) on stage 4 ....

In progress

8 We ......are still planning...... (plan) a new interactive website.
9 We .... (look) for more input.
10 They .... (work) on a website plan that will meet our requirements.

LANGUAGE FILE 1 >> PAGE 116

3 Communication activity

a **Work in pairs. Your company wants to launch a new product. Decide what the product is. Look at the stages and decide which are useful for your product, and the order you want them in.**

Make a large quantity of the product to sell.

Prepare an advertising campaign.

Ask people what products they like.

Make a small quantity of the product for trials.

Think of a name.

Ask people to try the product and tell you what they think.

Decide on the price.

Design the packaging.

b **You are in the middle of your project. Decide which of the stages are done, not done yet, or in progress.**

c **Prepare a progress report. Decide who is going to talk about which stages.**

d **Work with another pair. Take turns to give a progress report on your product, saying what you have/haven't done and what is in progress. Listen, take notes and ask questions if necessary.**

Progress report

1 Brief description of project
2 Outline – what the different stages are
3 Situation – which stages are (not) done/in progress

PART B Presentations

1 Reading

a Work in pairs. Look at this advice about giving presentations. Tick (✓) the advice that you think is good, and put a cross (✗) next to the advice that you think is bad.

1 Meet your audience before the presentation.
2 Find out about the room and facilities.
3 Write out the complete text of your presentation.
4 Prepare all your materials before the presentation.
5 Use as much different equipment as possible.
6 Rehearse your presentation.
7 Look at the same two or three members of the audience.
8 Smile a lot.
9 Use hand gestures.
10 Keep moving to different parts of the room.

b Now read this article giving advice about presentations and check your answers. Do you agree with all the advice in the article?

We all get nervous before giving a presentation, but follow this advice and you will find it easy!

Before the presentation...

- Try to find out as much as possible about your audience. Who are they, how much do they already know about the subject of your presentation, why are they coming and what do they expect to get from it?
- Ask the organizers about the room. How big is it, how many seats are there, what equipment and facilities are there? If possible, visit the room before your talk so that you are familiar with it.
- Plan your presentation carefully. Don't write down every word because if you just read to the audience it will sound boring; instead you should make notes which will help you remember what to say.
- Get everything ready well in advance, for example handouts, overhead slides etc.
- Plan what equipment you will need. Try not to use too much, as this will distract the audience from what you want to say. Choose the best equipment for your presentation, and plan to use it only when it will help to explain a point.
- Practise the complete presentation at least once. Ask a friend or colleague to listen and give you advice about anything that may need changing.

During the presentation...

- Make eye contact with your audience, but be careful not to concentrate on the same few people – make eye contact with many different members of the audience.
- You may feel nervous but try to look happy and confident. Smile at certain moments during your presentation, but not too much as this can make you look nervous and 'false'.
- You should use hand gestures to help explain some of your ideas, but again don't do it too much or the audience will be distracted from what you want to say.
- Try not to move around too much – stay more or less in the same place so that the audience can concentrate on you more easily.

2 Listening

a Mark Plewka is giving a presentation about ways of improving communication in his company. Listen to parts of his presentation, and number these things in the order that you hear them.

a conclusion ☐
b main body – three parts ☐
c name of presenter's company ☐
d outline – three parts ☐
e presenter's name ☐
f questions ☐
g summary – three parts ☐
h title of presentation ☐

b From what you heard, do you think this is a good presentation? Why / Why not?

3 Language focus

Listen again and complete the things that Mark said.

1 Good afternoon everyone, and .... coming.
2 OK, ... look at the importance of communication.
3 .... on this transparency, I asked some fairly basic questions.
4 So, ... look at what we did about this.
5 Let .... then. Firstly, we looked at ...
6 And that .... of my presentation.
.... questions?

LANGUAGE FILE 2 >> PAGE 116

4 Exploring

a Prepare a short presentation about one of these topics or another topic that you are interested in. Use Mark's presentation to help you.

your job	your workplace
one of your interests	your town

Remember to make a plan. Use this structure:
1 Introduction
2 Outline
3 Main body
4 Conclusion

b Rehearse your presentation with a partner. Give each other suggestions for improvements.

c Give your presentation to the group. As you listen to other students' presentations, make notes and ask questions at the end.

REVIEW 5

Vocabulary 1

Match the percentages 1–8 to the phrases a–h.

1 18%	a nearly a third
2 26%	b around half
3 32.5%	c just over nine tenths
4 35%	d almost a fifth
5 49%	e about two thirds
6 64%	f just over a quarter
7 75%	g exactly three quarters
8 91%	h just over a third

Language 1

Put this conversation in the correct order.

TOM:	Come on, she's free now.	☐
RENATA:	Yes, of course I am.	☐
RENATA:	Hi, Tom. Fine, thanks. How are you?	☐
TOM:	Hi, Renata. How are you?	1
RENATA:	Yes, I'd love to.	☐
TOM:	Well, that's Helen Gregan. She runs the local association of journalists. Would you like to meet her?	☐
TOM:	I'm fine. Are you still interested in meeting local journalists?	☐

Communication 1

Think of a project you are working on at the moment, in your work or studies. Make notes under these headings:

Done	Not done yet	In progress

Work in small groups. Give each other a progress report on your projects.

Vocabulary 2

Put the phrases with similar meanings into groups. (There are five groups.)

decrease a little
decrease a lot
fall sharply
fall slightly
go down a bit
go down dramatically
go up a bit
go up dramatically
increase a little
increase a lot
remain steady
rise sharply
rise slightly
stay the same

Language 2

Complete the predictions below using the words in the box.

hope	think	will	can	expect	predict

1 I don't .... to see high sales this year.
2 Profits .... probably fall in the winter.
3 I don't .... sales will rise as much as we would like.
4 I confidently .... that next year will be our best ever.
5 We .... expect profits to rise in summer.
6 I .... sales don't fall any more next year.

Communication 2

With a partner, discuss the following questions.

1 How many computers are there in your company/class now? Has that changed recently? How many will there be in the future?
2 How many people are able to use computers well in your company/class? Has that changed recently? How many will be able to use computers in the future?
3 How many of the computers in your company/class are up-to-date models? Has that changed recently? How many will be up-to-date in the future?

Choose one topic about computers and change, and present it to the class.

Communication activities

UNIT 2 PART A PAGE 11

4 **You are going to describe a company for Student B. Either describe a company you know or use the information opposite and describe those companies. Use the sentences from** 3 Listening b **on page 11 to help you. Do not say the name of the company. Student B will try to guess the name of the company.**

1 airline – biggest in Europe – France – 43.3 million passengers a year – 83 countries – Air France

2 fast food retailer – USA – 46 million customers a day – 30,000 restaurants – 118 countries – McDonald's

Now listen to Student B's descriptions of two companies, and complete the table.

		Product or service	Location	Size
1				
2				

Can you guess the names of the companies?

UNIT 2 PART B PAGE 13

3 **a Student B has some information about Airbus. Ask about Airbus and make notes.**

- when established?
- location?
- product/service?
- number of employees?
- annual turnover?
- philosophy?

b Use this information to answer Student B's questions about Hitachi.

- established 1910
- Tokyo, Japan
- manufacturer of computers and electrical equipment
- over 300,000 employees
- annual sales $60.1 billion (20,000 products)
- 'contribute to people and society through technology'

UNIT 7 PART B PAGE 37

4 **Situation 1**

Imagine you are Kate Delgado and you're listening to your voicemail messages. Write down the message that Student B leaves. Then check with him/her that your message is correct.

Situation 2

Leave a voicemail message for Barry Chapman, a client in New York.
You want a meeting in New York next month – you are going on a trip there. You will email your dates.
Ask Barry Chapman to recommend a hotel.

UNIT 3 PART A PAGE 15

4 **a** **Imagine that you are Kim Burke. Prepare to tell Student B about your job.**

	You	Your partner
Work for:	Dell computers – eight years	
Job:	Customer Services Manager – 2002 to now	
Environment:	Call centre	
Responsibility:	Manage call centre staff	

b **Tell each other about your jobs, and complete the 'Your partner' column.**

UNIT 5 PART A PAGE 25

4 **Situation 1**
Student B wants you to recommend a printing company. Listen to what Student B needs, then tell Student B about the companies opposite (price, speed, quality).

Example
Budget Print is cheaper, but Multiprint is better quality than Budget Print and offers free delivery.

MULTIPRINT
Top quality colour printing
Free delivery anywhere in the city
Fast delivery – 24 hours
Reasonable prices
Colour A4 sheet: €15 for 10
B/w A4 sheet: €5 for 10
Tel: 0866 542555

BUDGET PRINT
Colour A4 sheet: €10 for 10
B/w A4 sheet: €2 for 10
Delivery:
24 hours for black and white;
48 hours for colour
Call now: 0866 554646
Cheapest prices in the city – guaranteed!

Situation 2
You are organizing a conference for about 100 people. You cannot afford to spend too much on the conference room, and most of the participants will be arriving by train. Ask Student B to recommend a good conference facility. Talk to Student B and fill in the table. Then tell Student B which you think is best, and why.

	Price	Size	Convenience
Event Management Ltd			
Park Hotel			
Northern Hotel			

UNIT 2 PART A PAGE 11

4 Listen to Student A's descriptions of two companies, and complete the table.

		Product or service	Location	Size
1				
2				

Can you guess the names of the companies?

Now you are going to describe a company for Student A. Either describe a company you know or use the information opposite and describe those companies. Use the sentences from 3 Listening b on page 11 to help you. Do not say the name of the company. Student A will try to guess the name of the company.

1 express delivery company – USA – 220 countries – first air express company – 1969 – DHL

2 USA – invented cornflakes – breakfast cereal manufacturer in 19 countries – sells in 160 countries – Kellogg's

UNIT 6 PART A PAGE 29

4 **a** Explain to Student B how to use an office voicemail system. Use *if* or *when* and the prompts below to help you. Student B will make notes.

1 Change greeting → Enter PIN code.

2 Want to record own greeting → No – press 6 for standard greeting. / Yes – press 8 and say message.

3 Listen to new messages → Enter PIN code and press 3.

4 Hear a message again → Yes – press 5. / No – press 7.

5 Want to leave voicemail system → Press 9 and star.

b Now listen to Student B explain how to set up an email holiday message. Make notes.

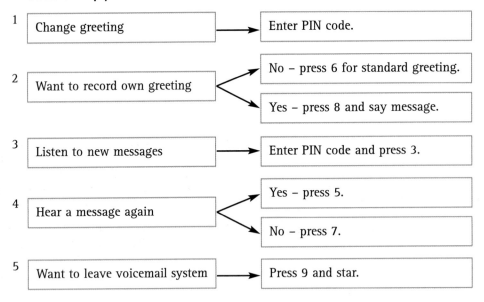

UNIT 8 PART A PAGE 39

3 You are Kim Wesley, the Catering Manager at the Sunrise Hotel. Student B is Sam Beattie, a salesperson for Smooth, a company which supplies soft drinks dispensers for bars. Student B calls you.

Look at your schedule (on the right). Try to make an appointment to meet Student B.

Monday 13
a.m. ....
p.m. 12.30 large group arriving. Supervise till 7.00.

Tuesday 14
a.m. 10.00 - 1.30 interviews for new bar staff
p.m. ....

Wednesday 15
a.m. ....
p.m. staff meeting 2.00 - 4.30

Thursday 16
a.m. DAY
p.m. OFF

Friday 17
a.m. 10.00-12.00 management meeting
p.m. ....

UNIT 9 PART A PAGE 43

5 Write an email to the others in your group, telling them when you are available.

Available:	Tuesday afternoon, Wednesday all day
Not available:	Monday all day, Thursday all day
Possible:	Tuesday morning, Friday all day

UNIT 9 PART B PAGE 45

4 You are the Marketing Director, and the chairperson of the meeting.

Look at the notes about the four agencies on page 45, and decide which one you think would be best, and why. When everybody is ready, have a meeting with the other senior managers in your group and try to decide on the best agency for your company.

You should start off by inviting one of the others to give their views about last year's advertising campaign.

Last year's advertising campaign: You think the agency was not very creative, and the advertising was not very exciting. Some people say that the agency was very expensive, but you don't think enough money was spent on advertising.

Agency for this year's campaign: It is important for you that the advertising agency is creative and comes up with an exciting campaign. You don't mind if an agency is expensive, if it produces good results.

UNIT 8 PART B PAGE 41

4 **Situation 1**

Student B will call you. Try to solve any problems and reschedule your appointment if necessary. This is your schedule.

Wed 23

2.00 meet Student B
5.00 presentation at Fosters

Thu 24

11.00 strategy meeting

Situation 2

You have an appointment with Student B. Your train is travelling very slowly because of snow. You think you will be late. Call Student B, apologize and try to reschedule the appointment. This is your schedule.

Monday 19

a.m.

p.m. 2.00 – meet Student B

UNIT 9 PART A PAGE 43

5 **Write an email to the others in your group, telling them when you are available.**

Available:	Wednesday morning, Thursday afternoon
Not available:	Monday all day, Tuesday all day
Possible:	Wednesday afternoon, Thursday morning, Friday all day

UNIT 9 PART B PAGE 45

4 **You are the Finance Director.**

Look at the notes about the four agencies on page 45, and decide which one you think would be best, and why. When everybody is ready, have a meeting with the other senior managers in your group and try to decide on the best agency for your company.

Last year's advertising campaign: You think that the company spent too much on advertising last year, and in particular the agency was too expensive.

Agency for this year's campaign: It is important for you that the advertising agency is not too expensive. Quality is not so important for you; the advertising should be 'good enough', but at the right price.

UNIT 9 PART A PAGE 43

5 **Write an email to the others in your group, telling them when you are available.**

Available:	Monday, Tuesday, Wednesday all day
Not available:	Thursday afternoon, Friday morning
Possible:	Thurdsay morning, Friday afternoon

UNIT 9 PART B PAGE 45

4 **You are the Design Director.**

Look at the notes about the four agencies on page 45, and decide which one you think would be best, and why. When everybody is ready, have a meeting with the other senior managers in your group and try to decide on the best agency for your company.

Last year's advertising campaign: You think last year's agency was not very creative. It was quite slow, and you don't think it tried to understand the design of your company's products and packaging.

Agency for this year's campaign: In your experience there are always small problems working with ad agencies, but you don't mind this if the agency understands what you want, can work quickly and can produce good advertising.

UNIT 10 PART B PAGE 51

4

Situation 1

Your company wants to order 50 new computers. Student B is a sales representative for Comlink Ltd.

This is what you want:

- 50 PCs with monitors.
- 15% discount if possible, but you will accept less if you can get a fast delivery.
- Delivery next week.
- Free service contract for two years, if possible!

Enter into a negotiation with Student B. You want to get the best possible deal. Make notes of your deal.

Situation 2

You are a sales representative for Delta Motors Ltd. You sell commercial vans. Student B is a customer.

- You usually offer 5% discount on orders of ten vans, but you can go up to 10% if necessary.
- You can repaint at a special price of €750 per van – it's usually €900.
- You usually need two months to deliver repainted vans, but you can do it in one month for a small extra charge.

Enter into a negotiation with Student B. You don't want to lose the customer but you need to make the best possible deal. Make notes of your deal.

UNIT 9 PART A PAGE 43

5 **Write an email to the others in your group, telling them when you are available.**

Available:	Thursday afternoon
Not available:	Monday, Tuesday, Friday all day
Possible:	Wednesday all day, Thursday morning

UNIT 9 PART B PAGE 45

4 **You are the Production Director.**

Look at the notes about the four agencies on page 45, and decide which one you think would be best, and why. When everybody is ready, have a meeting with the other senior managers in your group and try to decide on the best agency for your company.

Last year's advertising campaign: You think last year's agency was unreliable and slow. Some people say the agency was too expensive, but you think a lot of money was wasted because the agency was not efficient.

Agency for this year's campaign: For you, it is important that you can depend on the advertising agency to maintain their schedules and keep their promises. The quality of the advertising only needs to be 'good enough', and you aren't too worried about cost.

UNIT 11 PART A PAGE 53

4 **Situation 1**

You are a bank clerk in Rome. Student B is a customer. Use the information below to answer Student B's questions.

Exchange rates

€1 = R33.3 (Russian roubles)
€1,000 = R33,300 (Russian roubles)

€1 = ¥128
€1,000 = ¥128,000

€1 = A$1.7
€1,000 = A$1,700

Situation 2

You are a customer at a bank in Athens. Student B is a bank clerk. Ask to change €1,000 into these currencies:

- South African rand
- US dollars
- Swiss francs

Make a note of how much you get for each transaction.

UNIT 13 PART A PAGE 63

4

Situation 1

You are at a Doing Business meeting. You are a bank manager. On the other side of the room you can see your friend Lorna Watson, who is the General Manager of Picketts department store. You often play golf with Lorna, and will be playing again on Saturday. Start a conversation with Student B. Find out what he/she does, then offer to introduce Student B to Lorna Watson.

Situation 2

You are attending a British Chamber of Commerce meeting for the first time. You are a salesperson for computer networks. You want to meet people from companies opening new offices. You have just been introduced to Student B. Chat with Student B and see if you can help each other.

UNIT 14 PART A PAGE 67

4

Describe the information in graph 1 so that Student B can complete a blank graph. Then listen to Student B describe graph 2, and complete your blank graph. Take turns to describe and listen to the information for the other graphs.

Example

1 *Sales of single use cameras have fallen steadily over the last two years ...*

1

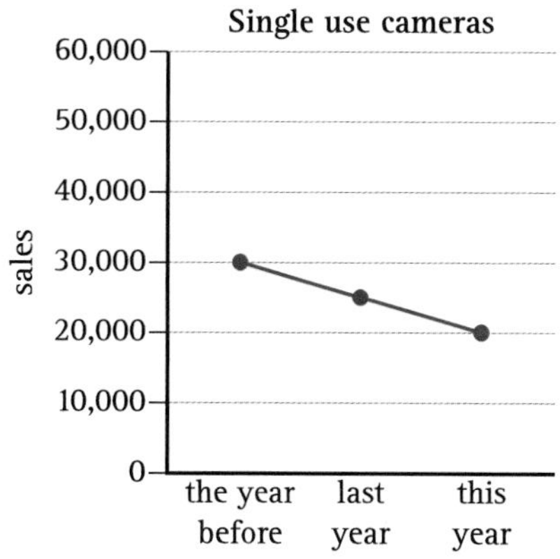

2

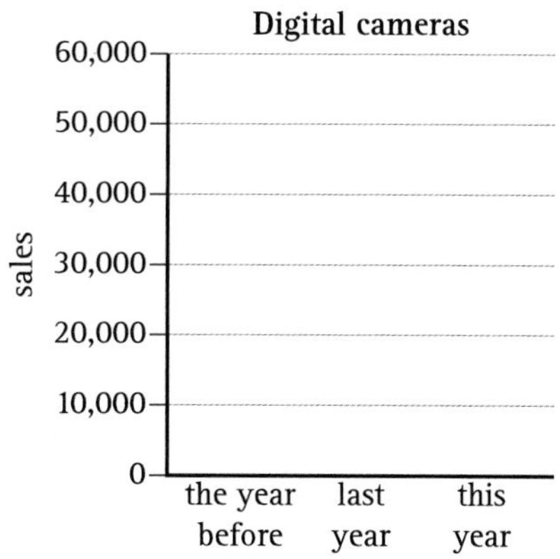

3

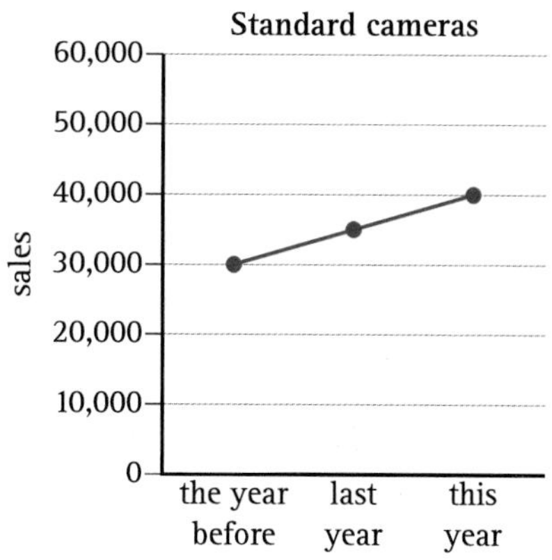

4

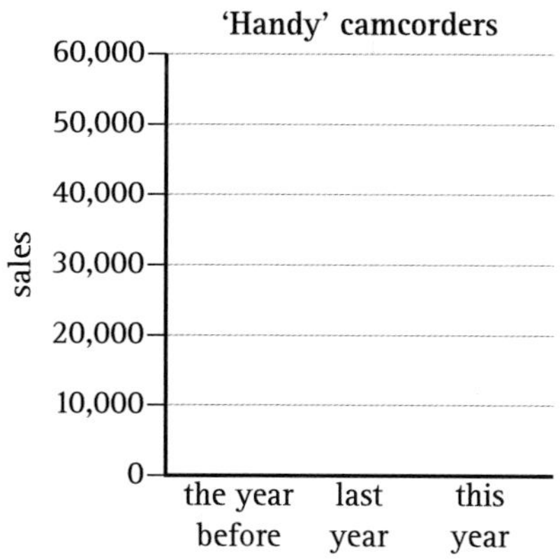

5

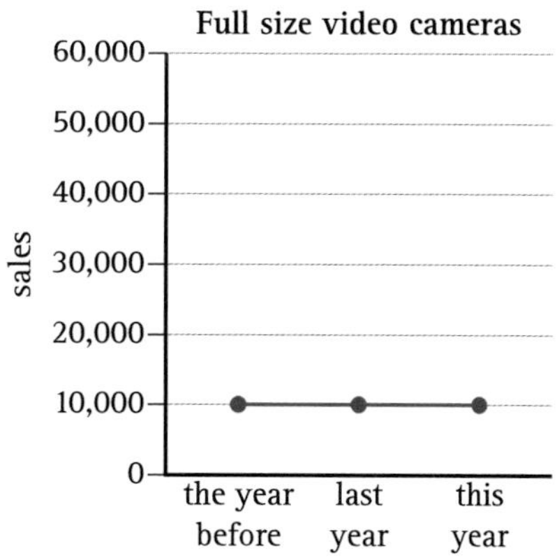

6

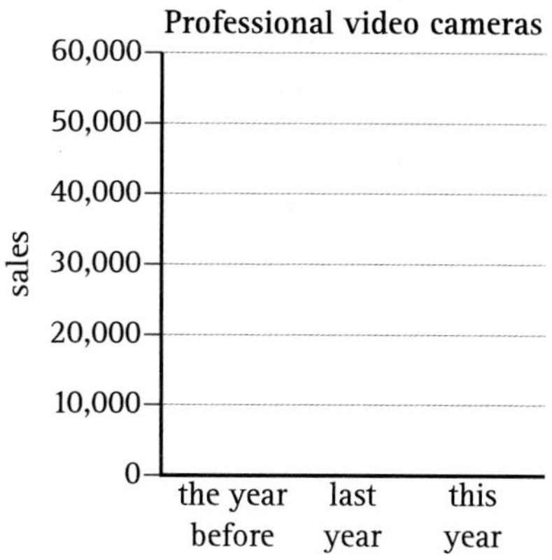

UNIT 11 PART B PAGE 55

4 **Situation 1**

You are a customer buying something on the phone. Student B is taking your order. Ask Student B questions so that you can complete the form below.

Bank transfer

Account name ....

Account number ....

Sort code ....

Bank ....

Bank address ....

Situation 2

You are a customer buying something on the phone. Student B is taking your order. Answer Student B's questions using the information below.

Credit card transaction

Card type:	Mastercard
Card number:	8636 753 951 852
Expiry date:	11/08
Name:	Your name
Security number:	378

UNIT 12 PART A PAGE 57

4 **Situation 1**

Your company is marketing a new mobile phone. Read the information below.

Aikon 246 mobile phone
Market: young business people living in the city
Marketing activity:

- Adverts in magazines and newspapers – easy to reach right market and cheaper.
- Billboards on main roads – cheap and effective.
- Not TV – expensive.
- Not sponsorship – difficult to organize (may be possible in the future).

Think about how to describe your marketing. Use these examples and ideas to help you.

- The product is a mobile phone.
- The market is young ...
- We're (not) planning to ...
- We've decided (not) to ...
- We're going to avoid ...
- We ...

Answer Student B's questions about your marketing.

Situation 2

Student B's company is marketing a new fruit drink. Think of some questions you could ask Student B about his/her marketing plans. Use these examples and ideas to help you.

- What's the product?
- What's the market?
- What ... planning ... do?
- What ... need ... ?
- What / decide ... ?
- What / avoid ... ?
- ... ?

Ask Student B about his/her marketing plans and make notes.

4 Listen to Student A describe graph 1, and complete your blank graph. Then describe the information in graph 2 so that Student A can complete a blank graph. Take turns to describe and listen to the information for the other graphs.

Example

2 *Sales of digital cameras have increased sharply since [2003] ...*

1
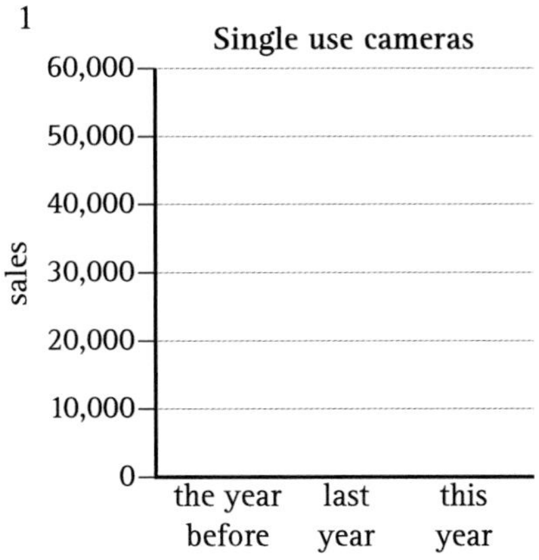

2
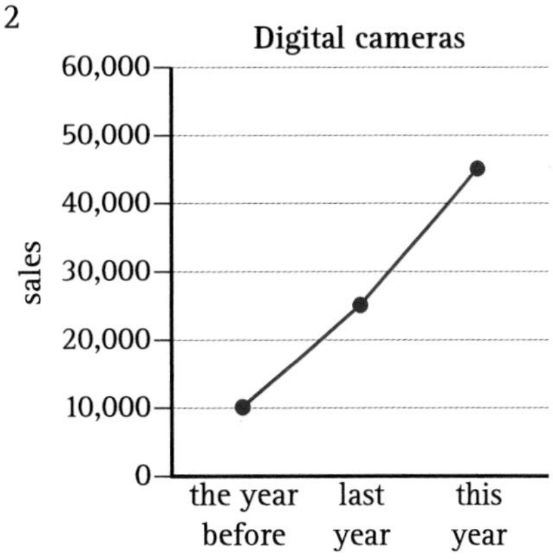

3
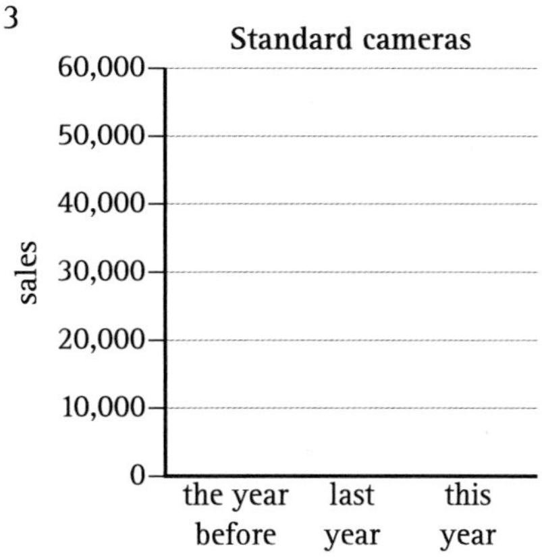

4
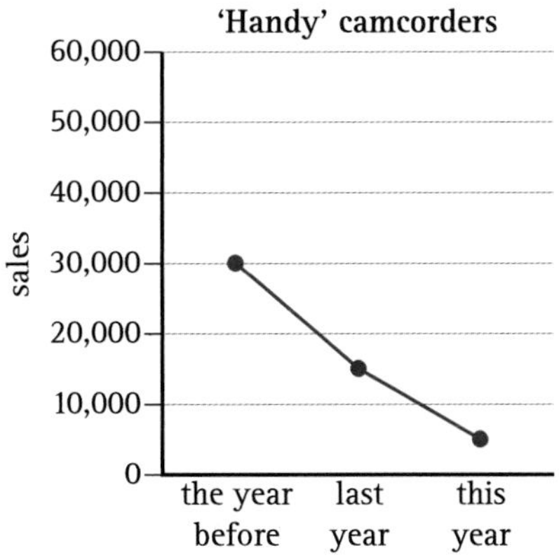

5
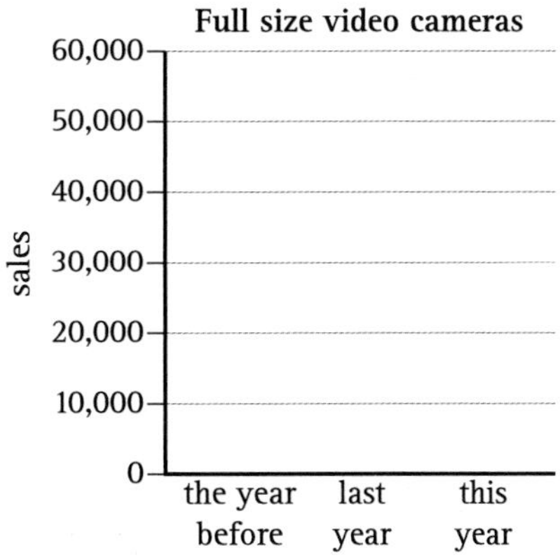

6
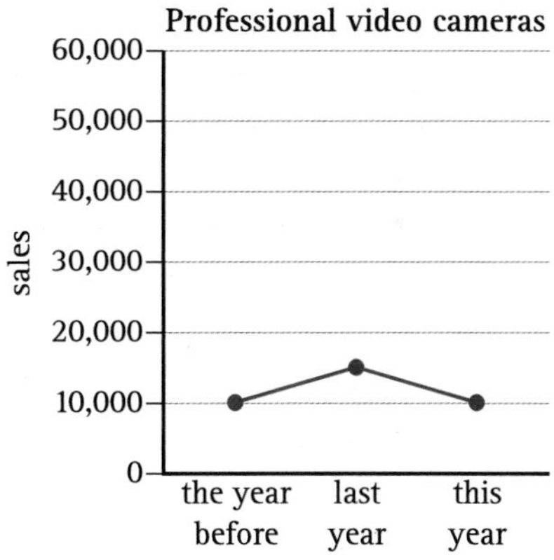

Help files

UNIT 1

Language file 1 Greeting visitors to your country

Introducing yourself	Responding
Hello. I'm David Smith.	
Hello, Mr Smith. I'm Susie from Mirage.	Please call me David.
I'm here to take you to the office.	

The visitor's journey

Did you have a good How was your	flight? journey? trip?

Do you travel abroad a lot?
Do you like travelling?

The weather

It's	a	lovely very	hot cold windy	day	today.

It's about 30 degrees.

People's jobs
What do you do in your company?

Offering to help

Can I help you with your bags?	Thank you. That's very kind. Thanks. No, it's all right, thanks.
This way. Here's our car. You can put your bags in the boot.	Thanks.

Put this dialogue in the correct order.

VISITOR:

a Thank you. ☐
b That's very kind. Could you take this one? ☐
c Hello, I'm Michelle Delon. 1
d No, only one or two trips a year. ☐
e Not too bad, thanks. Ooh. It's cold today. ☐

HOST:

f Can I help you with your bags? ☐
g Yes, of course. How was your trip? ☐
h That's not too bad. This way ... here's our car. ☐
i Yes, it is. Winter's here. Do you travel a lot? ☐
j Hello, Ms Delon. I'm Dennis Clark from Vista. I'm here to take you to our office. ☐

Language file 2 Present and past simple

Present simple

Use the present simple to talk about things you do regularly:

Do you **travel** abroad a lot?
I **do** about two or three trips a year.

and to ask and answer about your job:

What **do** you **do**?
I **work** in Accounts.
I**'m** a Marketing Assistant.

What **does** Sheila **do**?
She **works** in Administration.

Use the auxiliary verb *do* to form questions and negatives:

Do you **travel** a lot?
No, I **don't like** travelling.

Does Martin **work** with you?
No, he **doesn't work** in the same office.

Past simple

Use the past simple to talk about completed past actions and events at a specified time in the past:

be:	It **was** a good flight.
regular verbs:	Before that, I **worked** in Distribution.
irregular verbs:	Davina **left** last week.

Use the auxiliary verb *did* to form questions and negatives with most verbs:

Did you **have** a good trip?
No, I **didn't enjoy** it.

Why **did** you **leave** Amco?
I **didn't like** my boss!

but not with *be:*

How **was** your flight?
It **wasn't** very comfortable.

Put the verbs in brackets into the correct form of the present or past simple.

A: (1) .... (you have) a good flight?
B: Yes, it (2) .... (be) a good flight, but I (3) .... (like) the food.
A: (4) .... (you visit) this country often?
B: No, I usually (5) .... (come) here about once a year, but last year I (6) .... (come) four times, because we (7) .... (open) two new offices here.
A: Where (8) .... (you open) the new offices?
B: In Nice and Marseilles. It's hot today!
A: Yes, but you're lucky. It (9) .... (not be) hot yesterday; it (10) .... (be) very cold!

Language file 3 Present perfect

Use the present perfect to talk about past experiences when there is no specific time reference:

have/has + past participle

Have you **ever been** to Slovakia?
Has she **met** Bruce before?
Have they **seen** the new office?

I **haven't been to Slovakia.**
She**'s met Bruce.**
They**'ve seen** the new office.

Use the past simple to talk about past events when there is a specific time reference, or when one is understood:

I **went** to Russia last year.
I **met** Bruce in 2002.

Choose the correct word or phrase to complete these conversations.

1 A: *Did* / *Have* they visited our factory before?
B: Yes, they *have* / *has.*
A: When *did* / *have* they come?
B: They *come* /*came* in 2002.

2 A: Has she *saw* / *seen* the presentation?
B: Yes, she *has* / *saw.*
A: *Has* / *Did* she like it?
B: Yes, *she* / *she's* liked it very much.

3 A: Did you *heard* / *hear* the news about Alex yesterday?
B: Yes, it's very sad. I've *never* / *ever* met him. Have you?
A: Yes, I *did* / *have.* He's very nice.

Language file The passive

We use the passive voice (*be* + past participle) when we do not know who or what is doing an action, or we think he/she/it is not important.

Present simple passive

Subject	Verb	Object	
We	sell	46 million burgers	every day.
46 million burgers	are sold		every day.

Expert advice **is offered** to our clients.
Our products **are manufactured** in Asia.

Past simple passive

Subject	Verb	Object	
Somebody	started	the company	in 1925.
The company	was started		in 1925.

This car **was designed** in the USA.
Two new offices **were opened** in 2003.

We use *by* to say who or what does the action:

46 million burgers are sold **by** McDonald's every day.
The company was started **by** John Halley in 1925.

Questions
To ask about the first part of the sentence, the word order is the same as a positive statement:

46 million burgers are sold every day.
How many burgers are sold every day?

This car was designed in the USA.
Which car was designed in the USA?

To ask about the last part of the sentence, we use question word order:

The products are manufactured in Asia.
Where are the products manufactured?

The offices were opened in 2003.
When were the offices opened?

Put the verbs in brackets into the present simple passive or past simple passive.

The Cyclist's Friend is a cycle repair company. It (1) .... (start) by Nick Johnson in 2001, when he (2) .... (give) a small workshop by his businessman father. It is unusual because cyclists (3) .... (lend) a bike while their own bike (4) .... (repair). When Nick started, two bikes (5) .... (steal) in the first week, and one (6) .... (damage) very badly, so now cyclists (7) .... (charge) a deposit of €200. This (8) .... (give) back to them when the loan bike (9) .... (return). Nick also does mobile cycle repairs, so for example you can ride your bike to work and it (10) .... (service) at your workplace, while you work!

Vocabulary file 1 Word building

To make the noun describing a person or company that does something, you can often add the suffix *-er* or *-or* to a verb:

+ *-er*:			+ *-or*:		
design	→	designer	act	→	actor
import	→	importer	direct	→	director
-e → *-er*:			*-e* → *-or*:		
manufacture	→	manufacturer	operate	→	operator
			translate	→	translator

Match the definitions 1–6 to the nouns a–f.

1	A company which buys goods in another country and brings them back to its own country to sell.	a	manufacturer
2	A person who thinks of ideas for how to make something and creates plans for it.	b	retailer
3	A company which sells large amounts of goods to businesses which then sell to the public.	c	wholesaler
4	A company which produces goods in large numbers, especially in a factory using machines.	d	importer
5	A company which sells goods to the public for their own use.	e	exporter
6	A company which sends goods to another country to be sold there.	f	designer

Vocabulary file 2 Compound nouns

You can put two nouns together to make a compound noun:

travel agent
law firm

The first noun is usually singular:

car dealer
(NOT ~~cars dealer~~)

Some compound nouns are written as two separate words:

estate agent
furniture manufacturer

Others are written as one word:

airline
website

There are no rules about which compound nouns are written as two words, and which are one word, so if you are not sure you should check in your dictionary.

Note:
Some compound nouns are written with a hyphen in the middle but these are becoming much less common.

Make compound nouns with the words below. Use some words more than once.

accountancy	car	clothes	estate
computer	insurance	ticket	furniture
booking	law	travel	art

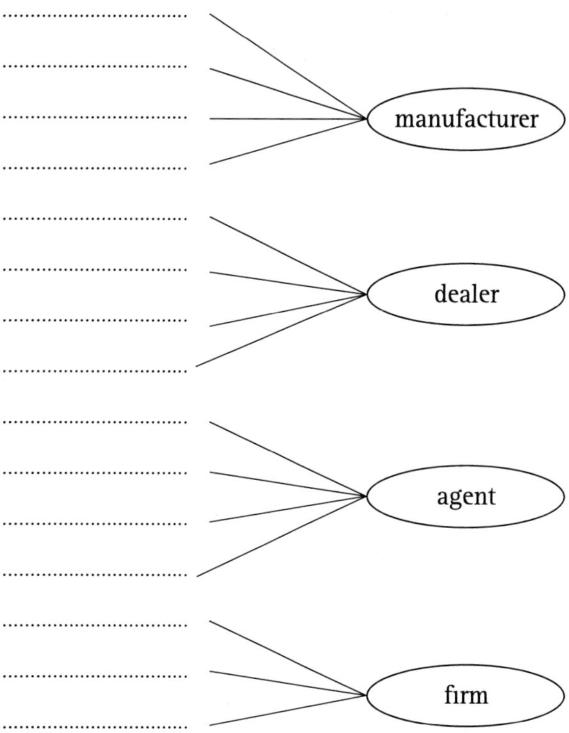

UNIT 3

Language file 1 Talking about your job

What do you do?	I'm a production manager.
Who do you work for?	I work for Espinosa in the production division.
What exactly do you do?	I'm in charge of / responsible for producing / the production of batteries.
	It's my job to ensure that ...
	I manage a team of five designers.

Language file 2 Present perfect + *for/since*

Use the present perfect (*have/has* + past participle) + *for/since* to talk about something that started in the past and continues up to the present.

Use *for* with a period of time:

He's **worked** at Avco **for** four years. / six months. / three days. / two weeks. / ages!

Use *since* with a point in time:

I've **worked** here **since** September. / 2002. / my birthday. / Friday. / I was seventeen.

Write complete sentences using the present perfect simple + *for* or *since*.

1 Ana / work / here / nine years.
2 Marcos / work / Madrid / 1999.
3 She / live / Paris / 2001.
4 We / work / together / eight months.
5 The marketing team / work / on this project / three weeks.
6 I'm hungry. I / be / in this meeting / 9.00!
7 My manager / be / on holiday / two weeks.
8 Steve / live / Germany / six months.

Language file 3 Talking about abilities

Use *need to, have to* + infinitive to talk about what qualities are necessary in a job:

To be a company director,

you	**need to** / **have to**	have	ambition.
		be	ambitious.
			able to communicate well.

You don't **need** / **have** to be qualified to be a waiter.

Do you **have** / **need** to be hard-working to be a doctor?

You can also use *need* + noun:

You **need** qualifications to be a teacher.

Use *can/can't* to talk about your own abilities:

I **can** speak three foreign languages, but I **can't** speak Russian.

Can has no infinitive, so we use *be able to*:

You have to **be able to** speak a foreign language to be a flight attendant.
NOT ~~You have to can speak~~ ...

Complete this job advertisement with the correct form of *need, need to, have to.*

SALESPERSON WANTED for FURNITURE COMPANY

Are you bored with your job? (1) .... (you/have) work in the same office every day, with the same people? (2) .... (you/need) a change? What about a new career in sales? To be a salesperson with us, you (3) .... (need) any qualifications, and you (4) .... (need) have any experience in sales, as we will give you full training. So, what (5) .... (you/need)? Well, you (6) .... (have) be confident, ambitious, and hard-working. You (7) .... (need) a driving licence and your own car, because you (8) .... (have) travel around the country visiting offices and shops. And you (9) .... (need) be flexible, as you sometimes (10) .... (have) stay away from home. But you (11) .... (have) pay for accommodation and meals – we pay all your expenses.

Call us for more information on 0807 8765432.

It's free – you (12) .... (have) pay!

Vocabulary file 1 Describing your job

Match these workplaces to the descriptions below.

factory studio office laboratory call centre

1 People don't realize what hard work it is — as soon as I finish dealing with one customer, the computer automatically calls my next one.

2 It's open plan, so it can get quite noisy sometimes, with people having discussions with colleagues at their desk, or speaking on the phone. It is friendly, though.

3 Because it has to be very clean, everything is white and it's quite cold. It's also extremely quiet, but it's not boring — we do have a laugh together sometimes.

4 I think some people have an image of paint everywhere, and an artist painting a big bunch of flowers — but in fact it's just me, my desk and my computer.

5 It's noisy and dangerous so we have to wear special safety equipment. Because we can't talk to each other, we often use signs to communicate!

Vocabulary file 2 Personal qualities

To be ...,	you need to **have** ...
ambitious	ambition
creative	creativity
patient	patience
confident	confidence
experienced	experience
qualified	qualifications
punctual flexible organized	(good) communication / computer skills

You need to **be able to** work (well) in a team. / on your own. / under pressure.

Replace the underlined words in these sentences with words from above.

1 Beat will get a job in senior management because he has a desire to succeed.
2 You need the ability to talk easily to anyone to be a business trainer.
3 Marina's a successful writer because she's so good at thinking of new ideas.
4 Pablo always looks very certain of his ability when he gives a presentation.
5 You will sometimes need to do a good job in difficult situations.
6 The new production manager is very good at planning and doesn't waste time.

Language file 1

Explaining needs

too + adjective:

This PC is **too old**.

not + adjective + *enough*:

The screen **isn't big enough**.

not + *enough* + noun:

It **doesn't have enough memory**.

Giving reasons with *so* and *because*

I need a new PC **because** this one is too old.
This PC is really old, so I need a new one.

Pronouns: *one(s)*

When we don't want to repeat a noun, we can use *one*, *the one*, *ones*, *the ones*.

Singular
My phone is broken, so I need a new ~~phone~~ one.
We all got new phones, but ~~the phone~~ **the one** that I got doesn't work.

Plural
Our PCs are too slow, so we need new ~~PCs~~ **ones**.
I think we need PCs like ~~the PCs~~ **the ones** in Accounts.

Complete the sentences using *too* and *enough*. Then match the sentence halves from A and B, and join them using *so* and *because*.

A			B	
1	Our Internet connection / slow		a	we should ask for up-to-date ones.
2	We need a new photocopier	so	b	these ones / not big / .
3	I think we should get new printers		c	we need to find a new server.
4	We need to ask for new desks	because	d	we / not got / seats for visitors.
5	The computers / old		e	these ones / noisy.
6	I think we need to ask for more chairs		f	this one / not fast / .

Language file 2 Talking about benefits

1 Explaining what the features can do for you:

The laptop has a big screen.	**This means** that it is easy to read. **This enables** you to read it easily.

2 Explaining what abilities the features give you:

Clear, simple instructions.	**You will be able to** **You can**	use the product quickly and easily.

3 Explaining what is not necessary because of the features:

Everything is included.	**You don't**	**need** **have**	to buy extra batteries or cables.

a Look at these benefits of a telephone answering / fax machine and correct the mistakes.

1 This mean faster transmission.
2 You don't need buy cassettes.
3 You will able to copy documents quickly.
4 This ables you to dial numbers quickly without looking in a phone book.
5 You not have to use fax paper rolls.
6 You can to send long faxes automatically.

b Now match these features to the benefits in (a) opposite.

a plain paper
b high speed modem
c 100 number speed dial memory
d 10 page document feeder
e microchip answering machine
f high speed photocopy facility

Vocabulary file Opposite adjectives

attractive	unattractive/ugly
fast	slow
flexible	inflexible
light	heavy
modern/up-to-date	old-fashioned/out-of-date
quiet	noisy
reliable	unreliable
simple/easy-to-use	complicated

Complete the sentences with words from the lists above.

1 The new photocopier is .... because there are so many different controls, but at least it's .... – 100 copies a minute!
2 Nina's fax machine is so ....; she has to change the paper roll when it runs out. She should get a/an .... one that takes ordinary paper.
3 It's great having a laptop with such a big screen, but it's .... to carry.
4 My mobile phone's so small and .... I often forget it's in my pocket!
5 Jerry's new printer is very .... – you can hardly hear it.
6 This is my favourite machine because it's really .... – I can use it as a printer, fax, photocopier or scanner. It's not .... to look at, though.
7 Our PCs are very ...., we've never had any problems with them, but they are quite ...., so you sometimes have to wait for documents to open.
8 My electronic organizer's very .... – I just turn it on and follow the instructions on the screen.

Language file 1 Comparatives and superlatives

	Adjective	Comparative	Superlative
One syllable add *-er*	*fast*	*faster*	*fastest*
double a single final consonant after a **single** vowel	*big*	*bigger*	*biggest*
don't double the consonant after two vowels	*cheap*	*cheaper*	*cheapest*
don't double the consonant if it is *w* or *y*	*slow*	*slower*	*slowest*
Two syllables change *-y* to *-ier* add *more, most*	*tasty* *boring*	*tastier* more *boring*	*tastiest* most *boring*
Three or more syllables add *more, most*	*expensive* *convenient*	more *expensive* more *convenient*	most *expensive* most *convenient*
Irregular adjectives	*good* *bad* *far*	better worse further	best worst furthest

Write sentences comparing these services. Use a comparative form when there are two services and a superlative form when there are three services.

Examples

Smithsons Buses €5, 55 minutes / Westons Buses €8, 35 minutes

Smithsons / cheap ...*Smithsons are cheaper than Westons.*...

Westons / fast ...*Westons are faster than Smithsons.*...

FlyByNight €100, 2 hours / SwiftAir €125, 2 hours / BigPlane €150, 1.5 hours

FlyByNight / cheap ...*FlyByNight is the cheapest (airline).*...

BigPlane / fast ...*BigPlane is the fastest (airline).*...

1 Europe OnLine €30, 28k / WizardNet €40, 56k
Europe OnLine / slow ...
WizardNet / expensive ...

2 ADL Bank 100 branches / Darcy Bank 200 branches / Bottings Bank 300 branches
Bottings Bank / convenient ...
ADL Bank / small ...

3 Northern Trains 400 seats, 5 hours / Express North Trains 200 seats, 4 hours
Northern Trains / big ...
Express North Trains / fast ...

4 Centre Hotel 2 stars, €100 / Town Hotel 3 stars, €150 / Beach Hotel 5 stars, €200
Beach Hotel / comfortable ...
Centre Hotel / cheap ...

Language file 2 Modifying adverbs

We can use modifying adverbs to make an adjective 'stronger':

The Clifton Hotel is	**very** **extremely**	big.

NHFC are a good airline, but they are **really** expensive.

Note: *Really* is more informal than *very.*

We can also use modifying adverbs to make an adjective 'weaker':

ParcelSpeed is	**quite** **fairly**	fast.

We can use modifying adverbs to show a big difference between two things:

Cybernet is	**much** **a lot**	faster than Webspeed.
Centrebank is	**much** **a lot**	more convenient than Suburban Bank.

We can use modifying adverbs to show a small difference between two things:

Western Rail is **a bit** cheaper than TrainWest.
SouthernLine is **a bit** more comfortable than National Rail.

Read this magazine article about an Internet provider and choose the correct modifying adverbs.

Webspeed have recently launched their new improved Internet service. I tried it for a week, and I was (1) *very / much* impressed – it is (2) *quite / a lot* better than before. The homepage is (3) *extremely / much* clearer now, and it contains some (4) *really / much* interesting articles. The connection is still (5) *fairly / a bit* slower than Cybernet, but it is (6) *very / much* more reliable than it was before – it can be (7) *extremely / a lot* frustrating when your computer disconnects ... And of course it's still a (8) *very / much* good price.

Language file 3 Opinions

Asking for opinions

What do you think?

Giving your opinion

I think a finance course is best.
If you ask me, a business letter writing course is best.
I don't think many people need to do that course.

Agreeing completely

I agree.
Good point (I didn't think of that).

Agreeing, but not completely

I see what you mean, **I suppose so,** **That's true,** **That's a good point,** **I agree up to a point,**	**but** it's useful for some of our employees.

Cross out the extra word in these sentences.

1 I don't to think this training course is a good idea.
2 If you ask for me, a computer training course is very useful.
3 That's a true, but it's very expensive.
4 I am suppose so, but I think a finance course is better.
5 I think of that we need more telephone skills training.
6 That's a good one point, but a team-building course is difficult.

UNIT 6

Language file 1 *if / when*

Use *if* + present for things that may or may not happen in the future:

I have to go out now. **If** my phone **rings**, just leave it as my voicemail is on.
(Maybe it will ring, maybe not – I don't know.)

If the line **is** engaged, try again in a few minutes.
(Maybe it will be engaged, maybe not – I don't know.)

Use *when* + present for things that will happen in the future:

I have to go out now. **When** Peter **calls**, take a message and I'll call him back.
(Peter will call – I know.)

For an outside line, press 9. **When** you **hear** the dialling tone, dial the number.
(You will hear a dialling tone – I know.)

Complete these instructions for a burglar alarm, using *if* or *when*.

First, unlock the front door and open it, then you will hear a buzzer. (1) .... you hear the buzzer, enter your personal code on the alarm. (2) .... you enter your code within 30 seconds, the buzzer stops. (3) .... the buzzer stops, press 'End'. The alarm is now 'Off'. (4) .... you take longer than 30 seconds to enter your code, the alarm goes off! Enter your code again, and the alarm will stop. (5) .... it stops, press 'End'.

Language file 2 *before, when, as soon as, once, after*

The time expressions *before, when, as soon as, once, after* can be used to connect two actions:

When I get home from work, I have a shower.
(= First I get home, then I have a shower.)

After I've had a shower, I usually make dinner.
(= First I have a shower, then I make dinner.)

Be careful with *before* – it goes with the second action:

Before I make dinner, I have a shower.
(= First I have a shower, then I make dinner.)

When these expressions refer to future actions, they are followed by a present tense (not *will*):

As soon as a delivery arrives, call the warehouse manager.
(NOT ~~As soon as a delivery will arrive ...~~)

Before you shut down your computer, log out of the system.
(NOT ~~Before you will shut down ...~~)

It is very common to use the present perfect with *after* and *once*:

After / **Once** | you've entered your PIN, you can access all your account details.

You can begin the sentence with either the first or the second action:
When you arrive, turn on the heating. (with a comma)
Turn on the heating **when** you arrive. (without a comma)

Make one sentence from each pair of sentences below. Use the time expression in brackets and make any necessary changes.

Example
Check the signature. Give the credit card back. (once)
Once you've checked the signature, give the credit card back. OR *Give the credit card back once you've checked the signature.*

1 The drawer opens. Then put the CD in. (when)
2 Press 5. Then record your message. (as soon as)
3 Finish copying. Then close the lid. (once)
4 Check the fax number. Then press 'send'. (before)
5 Visitors leave. Ask them to sign out. (when)
6 Switch on the machine. Then enter your code. (after)

Language file 3 Checking information

Can I just	check clarify	a few points with you? what you said about that?

Did you say that we should always check the credit card details?
I think you mentioned a discount scheme ...

Another thing was, I wasn't sure if	we need an email address. I have to call for authorization.

And just one last thing – how long do the tickets take to come?

Match the sentence halves.

1 Another thing was, I	a how much tax do they have to pay?
2 Can I just check	b customer accounts.
3 And just one last thing –	c wasn't sure if we need to see a passport.
4 I think you mentioned	d there are three ways to pay?
5 Did you say that	e some things with you?

Vocabulary file Using phones

pick up the	receiver phone

hang up
press the ... button
dial a number
redial

make an	internal external	call

transfer a call

dialling tone
switchboard
extension
direct line
outside line

engaged/busy

Choose the correct word or phrase to complete the sentences.

1 Can I make a note of your *direct* / *extension* line?
2 Chris's line is *engaged* / *transfer* – I'll just *press* / *dial* his number one more time.
3 Could I make a quick *outside line* / *external call*, please?
4 I'm having problems here. When I *pick up* / *hang up* my phone, I can't hear a *switchboard* / *dialling tone*.
5 Wait a moment, and I'll *pick up* / *transfer* your call to the *receiver* / *switchboard*.
6 We can only make *direct lines* / *internal calls* from these phones.

UNIT 7

Language file 1 Taking and leaving phone messages

Making the call

Beginning
Can I speak to Toby Jackson, please?

Saying who you are
Hello, my name's ...

This is Pedro Maya from DFD.
NOT ~~I am~~ Pedro Maya ...

It's Malcolm Hayward here.

Asking to leave a message
Can/Could I leave a message?
Could you give him/her a message?

Other action

I'll	call ring phone	again later. back.

Answering the phone

Getting information
Who's calling, please?
May I ask who's calling?

Can I have your	name number	(again), please?

Asking the caller to wait
Just a moment, please.
Can/Could you hold, please?

Connecting to someone else
I'll put you through.
I'll connect you.

Offering to take a message
Can I take a message?
Would you like to leave a message?

Explanations

I'm afraid (I'm sorry,)	he's/she's	not at his/her desk at the moment. in a meeting. on another call at the moment.
	his/her line's busy right now.	

Complete the conversation.

A: Flame Publishing. Can I help you?
B: Hello, (1) .... I speak (2) .... Sandra Selby, please?
A: (3) .... I ask (4) .... calling?
B: (5) .... Keith Atkins, (6) .... Belco Ltd.
A: (7) .... a (8) ...., please. I'm sorry, her (9) .... busy. (10) .... I (11) .... message?
B: No, thanks, it's OK. I (12) .... later.
A: All right. Goodbye.
B: Thank you. Goodbye.

Language file 2

Voicemail messages

Remember:

- your name and company
- name of other person
- short, clear message
- when to contact you
- how to contact you (email address / phone number)

For people you know well:
Hi, Dave. Chris here.
Hello Robert, this is Pablo.

For people you don't know well:
This is a message for ... from ... of ...
Please call ...

Let me know on 3838.
Can you call me back on 5536?

These voicemail messages are all in correct English, but they are not good messages. What is wrong with each one?

1 Hello, this is a message for Nigel Maws from Andrea Prodi of Delta. I have found out the information you wanted. Please call me back. Thank you. Goodbye.

2 Hi, Anneka. Have you seen the latest proposals on the intranet? Let me know what you think on 3361. Bye.

3 Hello, this is a message for Sheila Watson from Ray Baker. I'm afraid there's a problem with your order. Please call me back as soon as possible on 3449 609609. Thank you. Goodbye.

4 Hi, Juan, Mark here. This is what happened at the meeting. First, management said they couldn't change anything until next year, because all the systems have been established now. Second ...

5 Hello, this is Nina Gillespie with a message for Beat Schroeder. Could you please call me back on 8782 3309? Thank you. Goodbye.

UNIT 8

Language file 1 Present continuous for future plans

We can use the present continuous (*be + -ing*) to talk about definite plans for the future, when it is clear we are talking about the future:

What **are** you **doing** on Wednesday afternoon?
I'm seeing the dentist. **I'm** not **working**.

(NOT I ~~see~~ the dentist ...)

Complete the sentences with the present continuous form of the verb in brackets.

1 What time .... (Ms Kay / arrive)?
2 I .... (visit) the new factory tomorrow.
3 The managers .... (not meet) next month because of the holidays.
4 Terry .... (retire) at the end of this year.
5 .... (Mina / go) on holiday next week?
6 Carina .... (not come) this evening – she's too busy.

Language file 2 Making an appointment

Making a suggestion

Can I come and see you?
Could we meet next week?
What about Friday?
How about Tuesday?
Can you make / do Thursday?
How does Wednesday sound?
Does Monday suit you?
Is 10 o'clock OK?

Saying you are available

I'm free all day Wednesday.
I've got nothing in the afternoon.
I've got plans but I can cancel.
I can make / do Friday.
Tuesday suits me.
Monday's good for me.
Four o'clock's fine.

Saying you are not available

Well, I'm pretty busy this week.
I'm tied up Thursday morning.
I can't make / do Wednesday.
I have another appointment.
I'm out in the morning.
I've got plans. / something on.
I can't make it then.

We often use the present continuous to explain why we cannot make an appointment:

Sorry, **I'm interviewing** all day Wednesday.

When you say 'no', try to make another suggestion:

I'm tied up Wednesday. What about Thursday?

Complete these sentences with the words in the box.

about	can	cancel	come	fine	free	good
got	make	plans	see	suits	tied	visit

1 I can't .... it on Tuesday.
2 How .... Friday then?
3 Tomorrow's .... for me.
4 I'm .... up between 3.00 and 5.00.
5 I can ....
6 Can I .... over?
7 I've .... a meeting.
8 Thursday .... me.
9 I have to .... our Head Office.
10 I'm .... Monday afternoon.
11 When .... we meet?
12 .... you on Thursday at 5.00.
13 I've got ....
14 Six o'clock is ....

Language file 3 *going to*

When we know about the future because of information we have now, we use *be going to*:

I'm stuck in traffic. I'**m going to miss** my flight.
(Because I am stuck in traffic now, I know that I am going to miss my flight in the future.)

She's leaving the airport now. She's **not going to arrive** before the meeting.
(Because she is leaving the airport now, I know that she's not going to arrive ...)

What **are** we **going to do** about the problem?

Complete what these people say, using the correct form of *be going to* and the verb in brackets.

1 Oh, no, look at the time. I .... (miss) my flight.
2 Hi, we're stuck in traffic so we .... (not / be) there for 10 o'clock.
3 The weather's terrible – I'm sure the flight .... (be) cancelled.
4 Sorry, I'm lost so I .... (be) late. Can you give me directions?
5 I'm afraid the train's delayed. I .... (not / arrive) this morning.

We can also use *be going to* to talk about future plans. There is often no difference in meaning between *be going to* and the present continuous:

I'**m going to visit** our branch in Copenhagen next week.
I'**m visiting** our branch in Copenhagen next week.

We can use *be going to* when we have an intention to do something, but it is not a definite plan yet:

We've just advertised for a new Marketing Manager. We'**re going to interview** the five best applicants for the job.
(We don't know who they are yet, but that is our intention.)

When we have chosen the applicants and arranged a date and time for each interview, the plan becomes more definite and we are more likely to use the present continuous:

We've received thirty applications, and we'**re interviewing** the five best applicants next week.

Language file 4 Changing an appointment

Explaining the problem

I'm afraid	my	flight / train	has been	delayed. / cancelled.
		taxi is stuck in traffic.		
	I'm lost.			

Apologizing

I'm (very) sorry, but ...

Explaining the result

I'm going to be (a little) late.
I'm not going to make it (in/on time).
(*in time* = early or at the right time;
on time = not early or late)

Making a suggestion

Do you have time to meet me ...?
Can we put it back an hour?
Could we reschedule it for another day?
Can you wait for me?
Do you want to start without me?

Correct each of these sentences by adding one word.

1 Can we put the meeting back day?
2 I going to be late.
3 I'm afraid my train has cancelled.
4 I'm not going to make in time.
5 Can you wait me?
6 Do you want start without me?
7 I'm going to be little late.
8 I'm afraid taxi is stuck in traffic.

Vocabulary file Travel problems

There was a long **delay** because of a technical problem.

Our train was **delayed** for two hours.

The New York flight was **cancelled** because of bad weather.

Paolo's **running**	**late.** **behind.**	He's half an hour	**late** **behind**	at the moment.

The director's taxi's **stuck** in traffic. Shall we	**postpone** **put back** **reschedule**	the meeting?

Flavia didn't know the city so she **got lost**. She didn't know where she was.

Johnny's **lost** his car keys. They're **missing**. He doesn't know where they are.

Shirley **missed** the 7 o'clock bus and had to catch the 7.30 bus instead.
(NOT Shirley ~~lost~~ the bus ...)

Choose the correct words in the text.

The day of my job interview started badly when I woke up (1) *late / behind*. I got ready quickly and ran all the way to the station, but I (2) *lost / missed* the train and had to wait for the next one, which was (3) *delay / delayed* by twenty minutes. Then my taxi got (4) *stuck / lost* in traffic, so I arrived very late. But they said it wasn't a problem – one of the interviewers was (5) *cancelled / delayed*, so they were (6) *running behind / lost* and my interview was (7) *cancelled / rescheduled* for the next day. They tried to call my mobile phone to tell me but there was no answer. That's when I realized I had (8) *lost / missed* my phone! I think I left it on the train, and it's still (9) *missed / missing*.

UNIT 9

Language file 1 Organizing meetings

Explaining the purpose of the meeting

We	are going would like	to have a meeting	to in order to so that we can	discuss our marketing plans.

Checking people's availability

Can Could	you	give me tell me let me know	your availability for	... [days/dates]? the following dates: [dates]?

Can Could	you	tell me let me know	if you are available on ... [days/dates]?

Giving your availability

I'm free on ... [days/dates]
... [day/date] is fine

I am (not) available	on ... [days/dates] the week of ... [dates]

I can/can't make it on ...

I can/can't do ...

I'm not sure about ...

I may be able to do ...

Giving preferences

I'd rather (not) ...
I'd rather avoid ...
I'd prefer ...

My preference would be ...
My preferred dates would be ...
The best dates for me are ...

Confirming the meeting details

The meeting	takes place will take place is will be	on ... [day/date],	at ... [time] in ... [place]. from 9 to 12. between 2 and 4.

Match the sentence halves from A and B.

A		B	
1	Can you tell me if	a	discuss problems with the new products.
2	I can't make	b	your availability for the week of 21st January?
3	The meeting will	c	you are available on 13 June?
4	We'd like to have a meeting to	d	know your availability for that week?
5	I can do	e	take place on 28th November from 10.00 to 1.00.
6	We need a meeting so that	f	is on 3 August from 9.00 to 2.00.
7	Could you give me	g	it that week as I'm on a business trip. Sorry.
8	The meeting	h	everyone has a chance to give their view.
9	Could you let me	i	available on 3rd, 5th and 6th March.
10	I'm	j	15th–18th September.

Language file 2 Taking part in meetings

(See Unit 5 for giving opinions, agreeing and disagreeing.)

Inviting opinions; allowing other people to speak

What do you think?
What are your thoughts on this?
What does everyone think of that?
Does everyone agree?

Sure, go ahead.

Asking for clarification

Sorry, I	didn't quite catch missed	that. What did you say?

Interrupting

Sorry to	interrupt, stop you,	but ...

Note:
It can often seem rude to interrupt someone, so it is best to do it only when it is really necessary, for example if someone starts to say something that has already been discussed and agreed, perhaps before they arrived.

Asking to speak

Can I make a suggestion?

Can I (just)	say add	something?

Reviewing what people have said

Shall we (just) recap / go over what we've said so far?
Let me (just) go over that.
Let's recap.

Concluding

So, that's our decision, then. We're going to ...

OK, then, we all agree. Now	we need to ... someone needs to ...

Put the words in these sentences in the correct order.

1 go / just / that / over / me / Let
2 this / your / on / are / What / thoughts ?
3 catch / quite / that / I / Sorry / didn't
4 a / just / can / moment / interrupt / Sorry / you / for / I ?
5 decision / our / So / then / that's
6 suggestion / a / make / I / Can ?
7 of / that / does / think / What / everyone ?
8 I / add / something / Can ?

Vocabulary file Organizing meetings

prepare send out circulate	the minutes the agenda
organize book	refreshments a room
set fix	a date and time a finishing time a time limit
notify	the participants reception the canteen the restaurant staff
check	people's availability individual needs (directions, parking, special diet, etc.)

Complete the advice about organizing meetings, using the words above.

1 You should .... well in advance, so that you can fix a time that's suitable for everyone.
2 Think about how far people have to travel when you ...., then nobody should be late!
3 If you .... as soon as you know the date and time, it helps them to plan their schedules.
4 Everyone will know what time they can leave if you ....
5 .... as soon as possible, so that everyone knows what they will be talking about.
6 The meeting will be more enjoyable if you can .... which is large, light and airy.
7 Make sure you .... – no one can concentrate if they are hungry or thirsty!
8 It can be useful to .... about the meeting; then they will be ready for your participants when they arrive.

Language file 1 Negotiating with colleagues

Offering to do something

I'll ...

Do you want me to ... ?

(Maybe/Perhaps) I | can ... / could ...

Asking someone to do something

Can you ... ?
Could you ... ?
Would you ... ?
Would you mind ... ?

Perhaps / Maybe | you could ...

Do you think you | could ... ? / can ... ?

Do you want to ... ?
Are you sure that's OK?

Could I leave that with you?
Would you be able to do that?

Accepting a task

Sure.
No problem.
Yes, that's fine.
Yes, (that's a) good idea.
All right.

Rejecting a task

I'd rather not, if possible.
I'd prefer not to ...
I might not have time to do that.

Choose the best words in this conversation between two colleagues.

A: OK, let's look at today's work.
B: Yes, (1) *fine* / *good* idea. (2) Do you *want* / *prefer* me to open the post?
A: All (3) *right* / *fine*. You could open the post and I (4) *might* / *could* check the emails from the website.
B: Then at ten o'clock, (5) *could* / *would* you be able to go to the department meeting? I (6) *can* / *might* stay and answer the phones.
A: I'd (7) *rather* / *prefer* you to go to the meeting if that's OK – I need to speak to Mr Hollis if he phones.
B: (8) *No* / *Not* problem.
A: Are you (9) *sure* / *fine* that's OK?
B: Yes, that's (10) *sure* / *fine*.

Language file 2 First conditional

In first conditional sentences, the 'if' part is open – it is possible but not definite – and the other action depends on the 'if' part happening:

If you prepare the agenda, (This is a possibility – it may or may not happen.)	**I'll circulate** it. (This will happen depending on the 'if' part.)
If + present,	future form

The first conditional is used a lot in negotiations, where one action often depends on another action:

If you work extra hours this week, **I'll give** you a day off next week.
If I pay for your petrol, **will you give** me a lift to the airport?
If you don't order it today, they **won't give** you a discount.

The 'if' part can come second, but without a comma:

I'll circulate the agenda for the meeting **if you prepare** it.
I'll buy you a coffee **if you help** me with my PC!

Complete the sentences with the correct forms of the verbs in brackets.

1 If the phone .... (ring), I .... (answer) it.
2 .... (you / help) Paula if she .... (have) a problem?
3 I .... (close) the window if you .... (stop) smoking!
4 If Veronica .... (not / come) in today, I .... (do) those letters.
5 I .... (pay) for the coffee if you .... (pay) for the biscuits.
6 What .... (you / do) if Mel .... (not / finish) the minutes today?
7 I .... (call) all those clients if you .... (find) their phone numbers.
8 If François .... (be) late again, I .... (not / help) him at the end of the day.

Language file 3 Business negotiations

Polite requests	Polite refusals	Counter suggestions
We'd like delivery in three weeks.	I'm sorry, but delivery in three weeks is very difficult for us.	We can deliver in five weeks if we rush. Is this acceptable?
We'd like a 20% discount on this order.	I'm sorry. We can't give you 20% discount.	We can offer 10% discount. How about 10% discount?
Could you give us credit for 180 days?	I'm sorry, but we're not allowed to give 180 days' credit.	The maximum credit we can give is 150 days.

Agreement with a condition	Delaying tactics
OK, but if we deliver in three weeks, you'll have to pay extra.	I'll have to think about that and get back to you.
That's fine, but you'll have to pay for shipping.	I'll have to check with my manager and call you back.
Yes, but we'll need to do a credit check first.	

Put these sentences in the correct order to make two separate conversations. Start each one with a polite request.

a Could you give us a 15% discount on this order? 1
b We don't normally pay shipping costs. I'll have ☐ to check with my manager and get back to you. ☐
c I'm sorry, but we need three weeks for delivery. ☐
d I'd like delivery of this order in two weeks, please. ☐
e OK, 10% if we can have a one-year free service contract. ☐
f That's fine. I'll put your order through now. ☐
g Three weeks? OK, if you pay the shipping costs. ☐
h We're sorry, but our maximum discount is 10%. ☐

Vocabulary file Conditions

We can offer you a 10% **discount**.
Many shops **discount** their goods in January.

Smartco offer very good **credit terms** for big customers.
I usually get 30 days **credit** from my suppliers.
Trade credit is very important for small businesses.

If the heating breaks down, we have a **service contract** with the heating engineers.
We **guarantee** the quality of this printer. It has a **one-year guarantee**. If it breaks down in the first year, you pay nothing for the repair.
We offer an **extended warranty**. After your guarantee runs out, pay us €50 a year, and we will repair your computer free if it has a problem.

Next-day delivery – we will **deliver** your goods the day after you order them.
Shipping costs are 5% of the cost of the order. We always **ship** goods as soon as we receive payment.

Complete the text below using the words in the box.

extended warranty	guarantee	next-day delivery	credit terms	discount

We offer very good (1) .... – you don't have to pay for 30 days, and to reduce your costs we can give you a 15% (2) .... on large orders. If you need something urgently, we can send it by (3) .... so that you receive it in one day. Don't worry if you have problems in the first year, because we will give you a full (4) .... , and after the first year you can pay €10 a month for our (5) .... , which means we will continue to offer free repairs.

Language file 1 Numbers

Look at how to say the number 5,220,469:

five million, two hundred **and** twenty thousand, four hundred **and** sixty-nine
NOT five million ~~and~~ two hundred **and** twenty thousand ~~and~~ four hundred **and** sixty-nine.

We say *and* after *hundred*, but not after *million* or *thousand*.

We say some types of number in a particular way:

Credit card numbers

4329 3761 9481 7562
four three two nine, three seven six one, etc.
NOT ~~four thousand three hundred and twenty-nine~~, etc.

Bank sort codes (see Vocabulary file 2)

43-91-62
four three, nine one, six two
OR
forty-three, ninety-one, sixty-two

Bank account numbers (see Vocabulary file 2)

83721946
eight three seven two one nine four six
NOT ~~eighty-three million, seven hundred and twenty-one thousand~~ ... !

Phone numbers (see Unit 7)

8788 4061
eight seven double eight, four oh six one
NOT ~~eight thousand seven hundred and eighty-eight ... or eighty-seven eighty-eight~~ ...

Years

1994
nineteen ninety-four
NOT ~~one thousand nine hundred and ninety-four~~

2007
two thousand and seven

Writing numbers

We usually write a comma to show thousands and millions:
1,000 = one thousand
56,000,000 = 56 million

We put a point before decimals:
3.87 = three point eight seven
1.049 = one point oh four nine

Write these numbers in figures.

1 fifteen thousand, eight hundred
2 eleven thousand, three hundred and twenty-six
3 one hundred and seventy-eight thousand, nine hundred and ninety
4 four hundred and twelve thousand, six hundred and eleven
5 one million, seven hundred and twenty-three thousand, eight hundred and sixty-seven
6 two hundred and forty-three million, six hundred and fifty-four thousand, and thirty-three

Language file 2 Exchanging money

I'd like to | buy US dollars please, with | euros. / pound travellers' cheques.

I'd like to | change euros to US dollars, please.

Can I change euros to US dollars, please?

Is there a commission charge?
Do I have to pay commission?

How much | are you changing? / do you want to change?

Cheques or cash?

I'd like to / I'll | change 500 euros, please.

What's the exchange rate?
The exchange rate is 1.15 to the euro.
One euro is worth 1.15 dollars at the moment.
500 euros will buy 575 dollars.

Could I see (the cheques and) your passport, please?
Please sign the cheques.

Write complete sentences using these prompts.

A: I / buy / pounds / euros.
B: Certainly. How / change?
A: What / rate?
B: 68 pence / euro / moment.
A: / like / 450 euros /

Language file 3 Asking about payment details

Paying by credit card

Can I have the card number, please?
And (what's) the expiry date?
Is the card in your name?
What's the cardholder's name, please?
Can I have the security number?

Paying by bank transfer

What's the account name?
OK, what's the sort code?
And the account number?
Could I have the name and address of your bank, too?
And do I need to quote a reference number?

Paying by cheque

Can I pay by cheque?
Do you take cheques?
Who's it payable to?
Who do I make it out to?
And how much was it again?

Match these answers to the questions opposite. There is more than one answer for some of the questions.

1 11/08.
2 Yes, it is. CB Dwight.
3 56-11-89.
4 Sure. 615.
5 It's 5765 9031 8843 2981.
6 Ms C Grant.
7 98761234.
8 Yes, it's Central Bank, 180 West Street, Chapeltown.
9 Acorn Enterprises, please.
10 The cardholder is Thomas D Baker.
11 Yes, we do.
12 Er, $98.00 altogether.
13 Yes, you can. No problem.
14 Er, that's ... October 2009.
15 Yes, you do. That's EH/98302/99A.
16 I'm afraid we can't accept a cheque as it's over €500.
17 That's OK, we have a stamp with our name on it.

Vocabulary file 1 Currencies

Match the currencies to their symbols.

1	US dollar	a	$
2	euro	b	A$
3	Swiss franc	c	€
4	Swedish krona	d	¥
5	Turkish lira	e	Mex $
6	UK pound	f	R
7	South African rand	g	Skr
8	Japanese yen	h	SFr
9	Australian dollar	i	TL
10	Mexican peso	j	£

Vocabulary file 2 Banking

Complete the texts with the words in the box.

account number	card number	cardholder	cheque
cheque book	credit card	date	expiry date
PIN	security number	signature	sort code

When you write a (1) .... , remember to put the correct (2) .... on it – a cheque is valid for six months from then. Look after your (3) .... and tell your bank immediately if you lose it. It contains a lot of information about your account. The six numbers at the bottom on the left or the top on the right are the (4) ...., which identifies your bank and branch. Then the eight or nine numbers after that are your own personal (5) .... You may need to give these numbers if you phone your bank.

If you want to order something on the phone or the Internet, a (6) .... is the most convenient way to pay. You will need to give your (7) ...., that's the long one (usually 16 numbers) on the front of your card, the (8) .... – when the card will no longer be valid – and the name of the (9) .... You may also be asked to give the (10) .... , three small numbers on the back of the card. If you use the card in person, for example in a shop or petrol station, they may ask you to key in your (11) .... , or personal identification number. They will ask you to sign your name, then they will compare your (12) .... with the one on the back of the card, to make sure it is the same.

Language file

Verbs followed by verb + *-ing* or *to* + infinitive

Verbs followed by verb + *-ing*	Verbs followed by *to* + infinitive
enjoy Our customers say they **enjoy using** our products. *avoid* How can we **avoid spending** so much? *consider* We're **considering expanding** our product range for the next season. *practise* Please **practise giving** your presentations before the conference.	*want* People **don't want to buy** a product if it's too expensive. *plan* The department is **planning to increase** the marketing budget next year. *decide* We've **decided to use** TV advertising for the first time.
need (to describe what has to happen) Our marketing activities **need assessing**.	(to describe what someone has to do) We **need to assess** our marketing activities.
like We **like using** sponsorship when we can.	We **like to use** sponsorship when we can.
	would like We'd **like to use** TV advertising, but we can't because it's too expensive.

Complete the text with the correct form of the verbs in brackets.

Thanks for coming everyone. I'd like (1) .... (suggest) some changes to our marketing strategy. We're not attracting enough new business, so we need (2) .... (think) about how to bring in more customers. I've considered (3) .... (launch) new and different products, but first I plan (4) .... (increase) our market research budget to help us find out what people buy at the moment, and what they want (5) .... (get) from such products in the future. I think this research needs (6) .... (do) quite urgently, so I decided (7) .... (ask) you to carry out the first phase as soon as possible. Here are the questionnaire packs. Now, people don't always like (8) .... (take) part in these surveys, so over the next few days, please practise (9) .... (ask) the questions in a friendly way which encourages people to take part. I know, I know, it sounds awful, but I'm sure that once you've started, you'll enjoy (10) .... (do) it, and we'll get some useful market information.

Vocabulary file 1 Marketing

Good marketing means communicating about your product or service to people who may be interested in it – **potential customers**. You need to try and get your message across to as many people as possible – **reach a wide audience / get good coverage / get good exposure**. If you are using billboards, for example, they should be in the best place possible – a **good location**. However, marketing can cost a lot of money, and you will always have a **budget** – a spending limit – so you should try to **target your market**, that is, aim at people who you think will be most interested in your product or service. Then your marketing will be **cost-effective** – you will get as many new customers as possible while spending as little as possible – and you should **get good results**, that is plenty of new customers!

billboards – large adverts in public places such as the street.
direct mail – posting letters to people, with leaflets, special offers, etc.
print advertising – putting adverts in newspapers and magazines.
sponsorship – giving money to organizations such as a sports club to help them, in exchange for **advertising your company** – for example on a football team's shirts.
telemarketing – telephoning people to tell them about a product or service.
TV advertising – putting adverts on TV.

Choose the correct word in these sentences.

1 I don't think we should use *budgets / telemarketing* because it annoys people when you phone them at home.
2 Carlton Beer have signed a new *sponsorship / billboard* deal with their local football club, which will include their name on players' shirts and *sponsorship / billboards* around the stadium.
3 We really need to *reach / get* good coverage with this new campaign. We have to find as many *potential customers / budgets* as we can.
4 Bensons decided on *print / TV* advertising because it is a way into every living room in the country. *Print / TV* advertising is only seen by the people who buy that paper or magazine.
5 We felt the billboard site was too expensive as it wasn't a very good *location / budget*.

Vocabulary file 2 Websites

Match the words 1–6 to the definitions a–f.

1 link	a a list which you can't normally see on the screen, but which appears when you click on an arrow
2 menu	b a small image which you can click on, either to find something out, or (as a link) to go to a different part of the site or the Internet
3 drop-down menu	c a facility which allows you to look for certain words or phrases in a website or on the Internet generally
4 scroll	d a place where you click to go to another part of the website, or to another website
5 search	e a list of links to choose from
6 icon	f to move up and down the page, or sometimes from side to side

UNIT 13

Language file 1 Meeting people

Introducing people

Chris, | can I introduce you to Nigel Green? He's a new member.
let me introduce you to Nigel Green.

Nigel, this is Chris Tucker. He runs the Bright Ideas ad agency.
Nigel is going to open a new office here for Delight Yogurts.

Nice to meet you.
Good to meet you.

Finding out about each other

So, | what is Delight doing here in Europe?
what are Delight's plans here?
how long have you been here?
how long do you plan to be here?

And your job is ... ?

Finding/Recommending contacts

Who | should I talk to about ... ?
would be a good person to ... ?
can you recommend for ... ?

There are lots of advertising people in the football team.

You should | join – (it's a) sure way to meet advertising people!
speak to Jane.

You really must meet Jane.

There's someone you should meet.

Craig Tanner | should know ...
would be good ...

Come on, I'll introduce you.

Excellent. Thanks for the tip.
That's great.
Very helpful of you.

Put the words in these sentences in the correct order.

1 your / What / plans / here / are?
2 you / helpful / very / of / That's
3 I / Mark / to / introduce / you / Can?
4 open / to / factory / going / here / Star / are / a
5 would / to / ask / person / be / Who / good / a?
6 for / tip / the / Thanks
7 meet / should / someone / you / There's
8 you / Nice / meet / to
9 to / How / you / stay / long / plan / do?
10 must / Dan / You / really / meet
11 to / about / I / talk / Who / advertising / should?
12 meet / Good / you / to
13 you / been / have / here / long / How?
14 to / me / you / Joanna / Let / introduce

Language file 2 Following up

This is Neil Challis. We met at the Chamber of Commerce last month.
How's it going?
How are you doing?

I made a lot of contacts through the Bankers' Association, just as you said ...
I've made some good contacts, thanks to you.
I've met some interesting people.

I want to thank you for your help.
I just want to say 'Thanks'.
I'd like to return the favour.
I thought you might like to meet her ...
That's very kind of you.

Cross out the extra word in these sentences.

1 I've met me some very useful people.
2 I thought you might be like to meet Jonathan.
3 That's very the kind of you.
4 How is it be going?
5 I want to thank to you for helping.
6 We met us at the annual conference in June.
7 I've made up a lot of contacts through the golf club.
8 I'd like to return of the favour.

Language file 1 Describing trends

Past simple

We use the past simple to describe what happened in a past period that has now finished:

Sales **went up** in 2002 and 2003, but then we had quality control problems and sales **didn't rise** at all in the third year.

Present perfect

We use the present perfect to describe what happened in the recent past with an emphasis on how it affects the present:

Sales **have gone up** since last year, but our market share **hasn't increased** much, and profits **have fallen** because **we've invested** heavily in new markets.

Present continuous

We use the present continuous to describe a trend which began in the recent past and we expect to continue into the immediate future:

Sales **are rising** slowly; trading conditions **are becoming** more difficult because of new stricter laws, and new overseas markets **aren't opening up** as quickly as we expected.

Verbs

It's been a good year for us – sales are | **rising.** / **going up.** / **increasing.**

We are having a difficult year – sales are | **falling.** / **going down.** / **decreasing.**

We've had problems this year, but we're pleased that sales have | **remained steady.** / **stayed the same.**

Adverbs and adverbial phrases

To indicate a small change:

Sales have fallen/risen | **a bit.** / **a little.** / **slightly.**

To indicate a big change:

Sales have fallen/risen | **dramatically.** / **a lot.** / **sharply.**

To indicate a constant change:

Sales have fallen/risen | **steadily.** / **consistently.** / **constantly.**

These graphs show sales of six different models of car. The sentences below describe the graphs, but there are two factual mistakes in each sentence. Find the mistakes and correct them. (2005 is 'now'.)

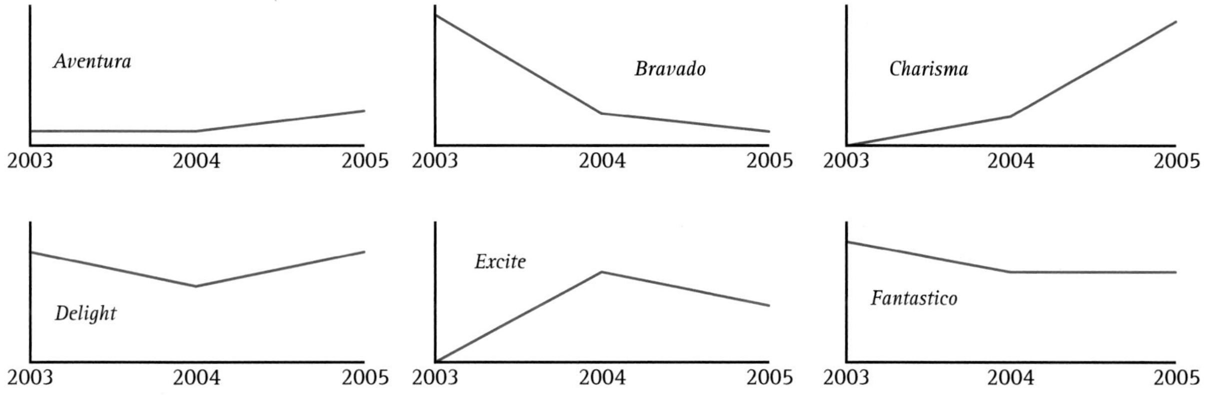

1 Sales of the Aventura fell sharply from 2003 to 2004, but they have decreased slightly in the last year.
2 The Bravado's sales rose slightly between 2003 and 2004 and they have remained steady in the last year.
3 Sales of the Charisma went down a little until 2004, but then they decreased dramatically.
4 The Delight's sales went up slightly until 2004 and have increased sharply in the last year.
5 After staying the same from 2003 to 2004, sales of the Excite increased a bit from 2004 to 2005.
6 The Fantastico's sales went down dramatically until 2004 but have fallen slightly since then.

Language file 2 Performance

Predicting future performance

I think profits **will rise** in the next three years.
I don't think costs **will fall** much, unfortunately.
NOT ~~I think costs won't fall~~ ...

Sales **will probably go up** a little next year.
Our market share **probably won't increase** much.
I predict that sales will increase sharply over the next five years.

I think we (can) expect tough competition from overseas.
I don't think we (can) expect an easy 12 months.

I hope we	**(can)** **(will)**	achieve sales of a million by 2008.
I hope we	**don't** **won't**	have the same problems again next year.

a Complete the sentences using the correct form of the verb in brackets.

1 We .... (hope) customers .... (not like) our competitor's new range!
2 I .... (think) sales .... (go down) slightly over the next two years.
3 We .... (not think) our competitors .... (expect) to increase their market share this year.
4 I .... (hope) our new factory .... (decrease) transport costs.
5 We .... (not think) prices .... (rise) much next year.
6 The company's profits .... (probably / rise) sharply in the next quarter.
7 I .... (think) our customers .... (expect) better quality in our new range of products.
8 We .... (probably / not make) any more of that model after this year.

Describing past performance

Traditionally, this is our strongest seller.

Between 2002 and 2004	we saw sales	increase. go down.	
	sales	decreased rose	slightly.

Sales have	been held	steady	at €500,000 a year.

b Write two sentences for each of these graphs – one describing past performance and one predicting future performance. (2005 is now.)

1

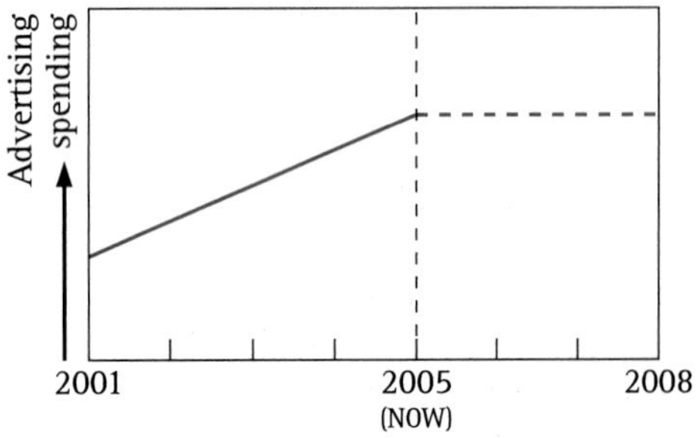

2

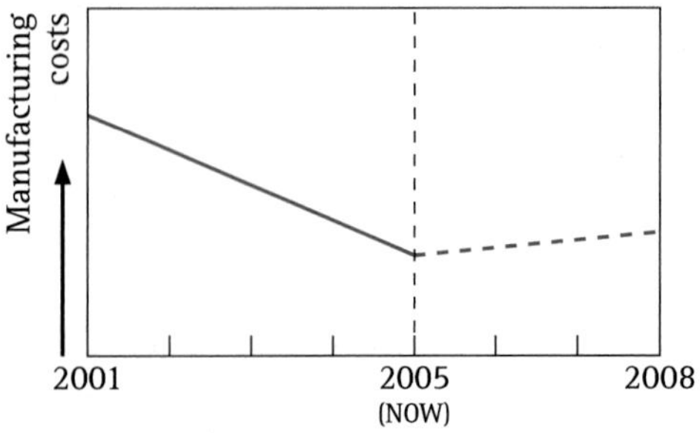

Vocabulary file Fractions and percentages

10%	ten per cent	$\frac{1}{10}$	a tenth
20%	twenty per cent	$\frac{1}{5}$	a fifth
25%	twenty-five per cent	$\frac{1}{4}$	a quarter
33.3%	thirty-three point three per cent	$\frac{1}{3}$	a third
50%	fifty per cent	$\frac{1}{2}$	half
66.6%	sixty-six point six per cent	$\frac{2}{3}$	two thirds
75%	seventy-five per cent	$\frac{3}{4}$	three quarters
90%	ninety per cent	$\frac{9}{10}$	nine tenths

Only **fifteen per cent** of the world's population has access to the Internet.
Half (of) the world's population is under 25 years of age.
A fifth of the population of Britain lives in or near London.

About / **Around** | **half of** the world's population has never used a phone. (= approximately 45–55%)

Nearly / **Almost** | **three quarters of** Britain's population has a mobile phone.

Just over two thirds of / **70% of** | the earth's surface is water.

Note:
We normally avoid using percentages with a decimal point in everyday English, and use a fraction instead.

A university asked 1,000 new students what experience they had with computers. The chart below shows the results. Complete the sentences using the information in the chart. Use a percentage or a fraction as shown in brackets for each one. Use expressions such as *nearly*, *around*, etc.

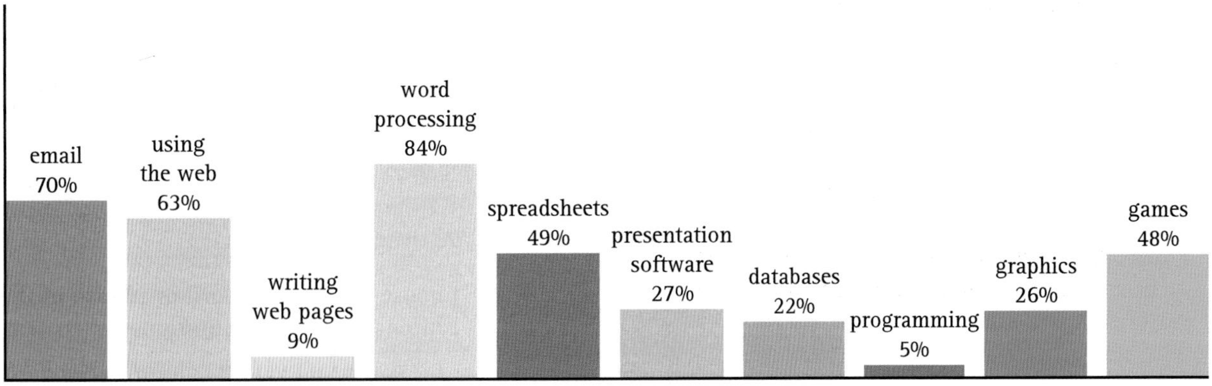

1 .... of the students have used email. (fraction)
2 .... of the students have accessed the web. (fraction)
3 Only .... of the students have written web pages. (percentage)
4 .... of the students have used word processing software. (percentage)
5 .... of the students have used spreadsheets. (fraction)
6 .... of the students have used presentation software. (fraction)
7 .... of the students have used databases. (percentage)
8 Only .... of the students have done programming. (percentage)
9 .... of the students have used graphics software. (percentage)
10 .... of the students have played computer games! (fraction)

UNIT 15

Language file 1 *already, still, yet*

Done (✓)

Use *already* with the present perfect to say that something we expected to happen has happened:

We've **already installed** a new phone system.
OR
We've **installed** a new phone system **already**.

Not done yet (✗)

Use *yet* with the present perfect negative to say that something has not happened up to now, but we expect it to happen in the future:

The new computers **haven't arrived yet**.
OR
The new computers **haven't yet arrived**.

In progress (...)

Use *still* with the present continuous to say that a process or action is continuing:

They**'re still installing** the new coffee machine.

Note: We can also use *still* with the present simple for situations which continue:

The old coffee machine **still works**.

Write complete sentences about a company which is opening a new call centre, using the correct form of the verb and *already*, *still* and *yet*.

Examples

choose location	✓	*We've already chosen a location.*
tell customers	✗	*We haven't told our customers yet.*
produce new stationery	...	*We're still producing new stationery.*

1	rent building	✓
2	decorate building	...
3	install furniture	✓
4	interview staff	...
5	write instructions for staff	✓
6	train staff	✗
7	organize staff restaurant	...
8	set up computer network	...
9	test phone system	✗
10	start advertising	✗

Language file 2 Presentations

Getting started

Thank you very much for coming.
My name's Robin Edgecombe.
I work for Stilson plc.
My presentation is called 'Internet security – a hidden problem'.

Outline

My presentation today will be in three main parts.
Firstly, ...
Secondly, ...
Thirdly, ...
Lastly, ...
Finally, ...

Main body

OK, to begin, let's analyse the problem.
As you can see on this transparency, ...
So, let's move on to some examples.
And that brings me to my next point.
I could say a lot more about this, but time is moving on, so I'll turn to possible solutions.

Conclusion

Let me sum up then.
Firstly, we looked at ...
Secondly, ...
Last but by no means least, ...
I believe that ...
And that brings me to the end of my presentation.
Are there any questions?

Choose the correct word or phrase in these sentences from presentations.

1 Thank you very much for *to come / coming.*
2 My presentation is *called / call* 'Difficult negotiations'.
3 OK, *to / for* begin, let's look at some figures.
4 As you can *seeing / see* in this graph, ...
5 So, let's *move / to move* on to some examples.
6 Time is moving *out / on*, so I'll stop there.
7 Let me *sum up / summary* then.
8 *Last / Least* but by no means *last / least*, ...
9 And that *brings / bring* me to the end of my presentation.
10 Are there any *question / questions*?

Transcripts

UNIT 1 PART A

1

JON: Hello. I'm Jon Wright.
MARIA: Oh, hello, Mr Wright. I'm Maria from Planeta. I'm here to take you to our office.
JON: Thank you. That's very kind.
MARIA: Er, can I help you with your bags?
JON: No, it's all right, thanks. They're not heavy.
MARIA: This way. Did you have a good flight, Mr Wright?
JON: Please call me Jon. Yes, it was a good flight, and very short – I didn't do any work.
MARIA: Never mind! Do you travel abroad a lot?
JON: Oh, about four times a year.
MARIA: Mmm, that's not too bad. Do you like travelling?
JON: Yes, it's interesting. What do you do at Planeta, Maria?
MARIA: I work in Marketing now, as a Marketing Assistant, but before that I worked in Sales.
JON: Right. Why did you change departments?
MARIA: One of the Marketing Assistants left, so I applied, and I'm very happy with it. Marketing is more interesting, I think.
JON: I agree. Wow! It's very hot today.
MARIA: Mmm, yes. It's about 30 degrees today. Hotter than London, I imagine.
JON: Yes, it is. How do we get to your office?
MARIA: I've got my car. Here it is. You can put your bags in the boot.
JON: Oh, thanks. How long does it take to get there?
MARIA: About 20 minutes. It's not far and we can take the motorway.

UNIT 1 PART B

2

1

CLAUDE: Hello. I'm Claude Mercier.
MICHAEL: Hello. I'm Michael Dunn. Nice to meet you.
CLAUDE: Nice to meet you, too. Please take a seat.
MICHAEL: Thank you.
CLAUDE: Have you been here before?
MICHAEL: Yes, well, I've been to France before ...
CLAUDE: Oh, really? When was that?
MICHAEL: Er, in 2003, I came for the National Conference in Toulouse.
CLAUDE: Oh, yes, I went to that.
MICHAEL: But I haven't been to Lyons before.
CLAUDE: Really?
MICHAEL: Until today! But I think it's a lovely city.
CLAUDE: Yes, there are some nice places to visit ...

2

CATHY: Hello, Jenny. Nice to see you again.
JENNY: Hi, Cathy. Nice to see you, too. How are you?
CATHY: Pretty good, thanks. And you? How are the kids?
JENNY: Oh, we're all fine.
CATHY: Good. Have you met Tom before?
JENNY: Yes, I have. Hello, Tom.
TOM: Hello, Jenny. I think we met at last year's General Meeting.
JENNY: That's right, yes. How are you?
TOM: Very well, thank you. How's business at the moment?

UNIT 2 PART A

3

1 Seatmaster! How much time do you or your secretary spend trying to book seats for those important events for your visiting clients? Sports matches, theatre productions ... Why not let us do it for you? Here at Seatmaster we'll make the phone calls, pay for the tickets, and even bring them to your office if necessary. Just tell us what you want, and we'll find it. We're based in London but we provide a service to businesses all over Europe, for events large and small. Just call Seatmaster on 08990 901901.

2 Globe Sports, for all your sporting needs. From one football shirt for your son's birthday, to a complete kit for a professional team, we can give you what you need. We specialize in football kit, and have factories in America, Spain and Turkey. We sell to shops through our sales network and to individual customers through our website. Visit us now at www.globesports.net.

3 Business is complicated these days. It seems that every day there is a new law related to business and the workplace. Hawes and Company can help you through the legal jungle of the modern business world. We offer help and advice on all the legal aspects of your business, from employees' rights through to international trade rules if you're buying and selling in different countries. With offices all over Europe, we can help wherever you are. And we're not as expensive as you might think! Call us free on 0808 663366.

UNIT 3 PART A

2

1 I'm Denise O'Connor. I work for an advertising company in Dublin. I'm responsible for all printed publicity material that the company produces, such as leaflets and brochures. It's my job to ensure that we give our clients the best printed advertising possible. I love my work because it's interesting and the people I work with are great fun.

2 I'm Derek Haslam. I work for an English toy company. I'm in charge of safety testing, so it's my job to ensure that our toys are safe for children before we distribute them in the markets. I manage a team of ten engineers, and each of them is responsible for a different aspect of toy safety. I like my work because I feel I am doing something important for a lot of people.

UNIT 3 PART B

1

KAREN: Peter, have you seen this job they're advertising on the company intranet?
PETER: No, what is it?
KAREN: They're looking for a new Marketing Manager in the tools division. You should go for it.
PETER: Are you trying to get rid of me? I'm not sure tools are really my thing, but what does it say about it anyway?
KAREN: You need to have at least three years' experience in marketing ...
PETER: OK, well that's no problem ...
KAREN: ... but you don't need to be experienced with tools, as full product training will be given.
PETER: Good! What else?
KAREN: Well, there are all the usual things, you know, you have to be flexible, creative, ambitious ...
PETER: Right, the usual 'super person'. Do you need to be organized? I'm not!
KAREN: No, it doesn't mention that, you're OK there! But of course you need to have good communication skills and you have to be able to work well in a team and under pressure.
PETER: Oh dear, definitely not me then ...
KAREN: Don't be silly – you can do all that, no problem. Er, what else ... you need good computer skills, er ...
PETER: What about foreign languages? Do you have to speak any foreign languages?
KAREN: No, it doesn't mention that, so I imagine you don't have to speak a foreign language.
PETER: Good, because I can't speak any languages apart from English, and even my English isn't that good.
KAREN: Oh, come on, Peter, you'd be ideal for the job – why don't you apply?
PETER: I don't know ... all right, I'll have a look at the advert and think about it ... when's the closing date?
KAREN: Er ... applications in writing by Friday the 29th of May ...

3

A: We need to make a decision this week about who to send to Mexico.
B: Oh, this week?
A: Yep.
B: Let's have a look at them again. Anneliese is the only one who can speak Spanish. That would be very useful. And she's very keen to go.
A: That's true, but she's only been with us for a year. Does she know enough about our products? I don't know. It's a risk.
B: Well, Chris has plenty of experience. But what about his family? He says they would be happy to make the move, but I'm not so sure.
A: I don't think we can let that influence our decision. Yes, he has experience, but he'll need to be flexible. Is he? I'm also concerned that he can't speak any other languages. How do we know he'll be able to learn Spanish?
B: Mmm, good point. Well, that leaves Jeff. He can't speak Spanish, but he's good at languages so we know he can learn.
A: He has three and a half years' experience. Do you think that's enough?
B: Yes, I think so. He's very familiar with the whole product range and he has excellent communication skills. I think he's the best choice.
A: I agree. Shall we call him up here to let him know?
B: Yes, I'll get my secretary to do it right away ...

UNIT 4 PART A

3 OFFICE MANAGER: Thanks for coming down to see me today.

FACILITIES MANAGER: No problem. OK, tell me what you need and we'll take it from there.

OM: Good. Well, first of all, a lot of the staff are asking for a new photocopier.

FM: Oh? Are there problems with the one you've got at the moment?

OM: Well, we produce a lot of very long reports in our department, and everybody says when they have to wait for 100 pages for example, it's just too slow. It is quite old – we've had it for about eight years, I think.

FM: Yes, I can see the problem. Right, I'll check the cost of a faster machine.

OM: That would be great. Also, I think we need new desks. At the moment there isn't any space to work because the computer, monitor and keyboard take up all the desk space. The desks aren't big enough.

FM: OK, I can find out about bigger desks ... is there anything else?

OM: Just one more thing. Could we get a new printer?

FM: What's the problem with the printer, is it too slow?

OM: No, I don't think it's too slow, but it's too noisy. Is it possible to get a quieter one?

FM: I'll talk to our suppliers. If you leave all this with me, I'll get some costs and speak to you next week. Is that OK?

OM: That's fine. Thanks very much.

UNIT 4 PART B

1 a When describing a product to their customers, a lot of salespeople talk about the features; these are the important parts of a product. But it isn't enough simply to describe the features – you also need to describe the benefits, that is, why the features are important for the customer. A product may have a lot of interesting features, but these are only good if they bring benefits to the customer.

b Let's look at an example. Here is an advertisement for presentation software, which lists its key features. It says that it's easy to use and up-to-date, and when you're preparing your presentation you will find it flexible. Then, when you're giving your presentation, the software is attractive to look at, fast and reliable. All useful information about the product, but does it help the customer? The customer is thinking, 'That all sounds very good, but is it useful for me? Do I really want or need to buy this?'

c If we explain the benefits of each of the features, the customer will understand the product better and can see why the features are useful. Firstly, the software is easy to use. This means that you'll be able to create great presentations straight away. You don't need to spend hours learning how to use it. That's a benefit. It's up-to-date, which enables you to use it with most modern computers. And it's flexible, so you can easily change things when you're preparing – a real benefit.

The software is attractive to look at, so here is another benefit – you'll create a better impression with your customers or colleagues. It's fast, so there is the obvious benefit that you don't have to wait a long time for each image to appear. And it's reliable, which gives a really important benefit – it won't suddenly stop working in the middle of your presentation, which would be difficult for you, and would create a bad impression.

So, by explaining both the features and the benefits, you will give your customer a real understanding of why the product is good for him or her.

UNIT 5 PART A

2 BEN: Judy, sorry to bother you. Do you know a good express delivery service?

JUDY: Well, Delivery Force are very good. They are the company we usually use.

BEN: I know. But I need to get this document to Vienna by tomorrow morning. What about Royal Star?

JUDY: Royal Star are really expensive. But yes, they guarantee delivery by 10 o'clock the next morning. Delivery Force are much cheaper and they'll probably deliver it in the morning, anyway.

BEN: I think I'll use Royal Star. It's safer. I must get this document to Vienna on time. Thanks, Judy.

JUDY: No problem.

UNIT 5 PART B

1

A: So, we have to decide between two suggestions: the computer skills course and the time-management course. What do you think?

B: I think a computer course is best. The market for computer skills is very big, because all businesses use computers these days.

A: I see what you mean, but a lot of people can already use them, so they don't need a training course. If you ask me, a time-management course is best. Employees can use those skills in every part of their job, and it's very good for their company, too.

B: Mmm, I suppose so, but I don't think employees will think it's very useful.

A: Good point – I didn't think of that. Well, as part of the course, we should try to help them see the benefits. This is a difficult decision – perhaps we should ask the trainers for their views.

B: Yes, I agree. Let's see what they think.

UNIT 6 PART A

2

MALCOLM: This phone system is very different to the one at my last company.

DIANA: Oh, don't worry, it's really simple, actually. Let me show you the basics.

MALCOLM: OK, thanks.

DIANA: First, if you want to make an internal call, press INT and then dial the extension.

MALCOLM: OK, so INT means 'internal'?

DIANA: That's right. For example, to call me, press INT and dial 3384, my extension.

MALCOLM: Right. That's easy enough!

DIANA: Now, if you want to make an external call, press 9 and wait for the dialling tone. When you hear the dialling tone, dial the number.

MALCOLM: Aha. Now, um, to answer the phone, I just pick it up, right?

DIANA: Yeah, when the phone rings, just answer it – you don't need to press anything.

MALCOLM: But what about transferring an outside caller to a colleague in the company?

DIANA: Right. You need to press INT again, dial the extension and wait. If your colleague answers, explain that there's an external call, and hang up. The caller and your colleague can then speak to each other. If your colleague doesn't answer, press INT to return to the outside caller.

MALCOLM: Great. You're right, it is fairly simple! Thanks.

DIANA: That's OK. Oh, just one more thing. To call reception ...

UNIT 6 PART B

2

NEIL: Tonya, after your training session yesterday I read the instructions on booking an airline ticket ...

TONYA: Good. Is it all clear?

NEIL: Yes, most of it. But can I just check a few things with you?

TONYA: Sure.

NEIL: Well, first, did you say that we need the exact number of passengers before we check availability?

TONYA: Yes, we do, because we need to check that the airline has the right number of seats available on a particular flight.

NEIL: OK, fine. Another thing was, I wasn't sure if we should ask customers if they have a preferred airline.

TONYA: No, we don't do that. People usually want the cheapest flight, and if they aren't happy with the airline we offer them, they tell us.

NEIL: Right. And I think you mentioned taking the customer's phone number – is that really important?

TONYA: Yes, that's very important, because we may need to contact them quickly if there are any problems.

NEIL: What about credit cards? Can I just clarify what you said about that?

TONYA: Yes, of course.

NEIL: Is a credit card necessary or can they pay in other ways?

TONYA: No, it's not necessary – obviously they can pay by cash or cheque. But if they're on the phone, we can't confirm the reservation until we receive payment.

NEIL: OK, thanks. And just one last thing – do we always post tickets to customers?

TONYA: No. Some customers prefer to come in and collect them – maybe because they're travelling very soon, or just because they're coming into town, anyway. But actually, we do post most tickets.

NEIL: That's great, thanks very much, Tonya.

TONYA: No problem. If you have any more questions, just ask.

UNIT 7 PART A

1

1

RECEPTIONIST: BST, can I help you?
TONY: Hello, can I speak to Martin Keller, please?
RECEPTIONIST: Can I have your name, please?
TONY: It's Tony Markham, from Leisure Plus.
RECEPTIONIST: Just a moment, please. I'll put you through.
TONY: Thanks.
RECEPTIONIST: Sorry, his line's busy right now. Can you hold, please?
TONY: Yes, of course.

2

RECEPTIONIST: Sonica, good afternoon.
TONY: Hello, can I speak to Nadia Gomez, please?
RECEPTIONIST: I'm afraid she's not here today. Can I take a message?
TONY: Yes, please. This is Tony Markham, from Leisure Plus.
RECEPTIONIST: Could you spell your surname, please?
TONY: Yes, it's M – A – R – K – H – A – M.
RECEPTIONIST: Thank you.
TONY: Can you tell her I'll email the information she wanted?
RECEPTIONIST: Sure, no problem.
TONY: Thank you. Bye.
RECEPTIONIST: Goodbye.

3

RECEPTIONIST: Megaboard, Steph speaking. Can I help you?
TONY: Hello, can I speak to Adam Kane, please?
RECEPTIONIST: May I ask who's calling?
TONY: It's Tony Markham, from Leisure Plus.
RECEPTIONIST: He's not at his desk at the moment. Would you like to leave a message?
TONY: No, that's OK, thanks, I'll call again later.
RECEPTIONIST: All right. Thank you for calling.
TONY: Thank you. Bye.

3

1

RECEPTIONIST: Century Finance, Paul speaking. Can I help you?
SARAH: Hello. Can I speak to Tim Banks, please?
RECEPTIONIST: I'm afraid he's not at his desk at the moment. Would you like to leave a message?
SARAH: Yes, please. This is Sarah Leigh ...
RECEPTIONIST: Can you spell Leigh for me, please?
SARAH: It's L - E - I - G - H.
RECEPTIONIST: Thanks.
SARAH: I have an appointment with Mr Banks tomorrow, but I need to cancel it. Can you ask him to call me, please?
RECEPTIONIST: OK. Can I have your number?
SARAH: Yes, it's 035 6478 9675.
RECEPTIONIST: 035 6478 9675. Thank you. I'll give Tim your message.
SARAH: Thank you very much.
RECEPTIONIST: You're welcome. Bye.
SARAH: Bye.

2

RECEPTIONIST: Good morning, Diamond Glaze. Can I help you?
CARL: Hello. Can I speak to Donald, please?
RECEPTIONIST: I'm afraid Donald's out this morning. May I ask who's calling?
CARL: It's Carl Phillips, that's Carl with a C, and Phillips is P – H – I – L – L – I – P – S. I'll call again this afternoon.
RECEPTIONIST: All right. Can I have your number anyway?
CARL: Yes, it's 066 8580 3491.
RECEPTIONIST: 066 8580 3491. OK. I'll tell him you called.
CARL: Thanks. Bye.
RECEPTIONIST: Goodbye.

UNIT 7 PART B

2

1 Hi, Bob. Roger here. I've looked at the designs and I think I'm ready to decide. Can you come to my office tomorrow to discuss them? Let me know on 8993. Bye.

2 Hello. This is a message for Lena Sampson from Emily Plessey of Net Solutions, telephone 337 8021. I've emailed the proposal you asked for. I'll call again later this week when you've had a chance to look at it. I hope that's OK. Goodbye.

3 Hello Jamie, this is Marlies. How are you? I haven't heard from you about the results of the survey. Can you call me back on 5536? The sales team is anxious to get the data. Thanks. Bye.

UNIT 8 PART A

1 a

TARA: Hello, Tara Luckman.
JENNY: Hello, Tara. This is Jenny Young from BK Plastics.
TARA: Hi, Jenny. How are you?
JENNY: Fine, thanks, and you?
TARA: Very well. What can I do for you?
JENNY: We've got some new products which I think you might be interested in.
TARA: OK.
JENNY: Can I come and see you this week to show you what we've got?
TARA: Well, I'm pretty busy this week, but ... let me look at my diary ... OK.
JENNY: I'm free all day Wednesday.
TARA: Sorry, Jenny, I'm interviewing all day Wednesday ... but I'm free all day Thursday.
JENNY: Ah, I'm tied up Thursday morning and I have another appointment on Thursday afternoon.
TARA: What about Friday? I'm out in the morning but I've got nothing in the afternoon.
JENNY: Let me see ... I've got plans but I can cancel ... and I'm visiting another client in the morning so I could come straight to you in the afternoon. Is two o'clock OK?
TARA: Two o'clock's fine.
JENNY: Great. OK ... see you on Friday then.
TARA: Thanks, Jenny. See you then.
JENNY: Bye.
TARA: Bye.

b

1

JENNY: I'm free all day Wednesday.
TARA: Sorry, Jenny, I'm interviewing all day Wednesday ... but I'm free all day Thursday.

2

JENNY: Let me see ... I've got plans but I can cancel ... and I'm visiting another client in the morning so I could come straight to you in the afternoon. Is two o'clock OK?

UNIT 8 PART B

2 b

RECEPTIONIST: Good morning. Mullins.
SOPHIE: Hello. This is Sophie Mueller of Deutsche Telecom. Is Mr Cho in the office?
RECEPTIONIST: Just a moment, Ms Mueller. I'll check. ... Ms Mueller?
SOPHIE: Yes?
RECEPTIONIST: I'll put you through.
SOPHIE: Thanks.
FRANK: Hello, Ms Mueller. How are you?
SOPHIE: Fine, thank you ... but ... uh ... I'm afraid my flight has been delayed. I'm sorry, but I'm not going to make it to Seoul in time for our appointment.
FRANK: Oh, dear. How long is the delay?
SOPHIE: They say two hours, but most of the flights are delayed. I think it's going to be longer than that.
FRANK: Oh, that's a shame. Well, shall we reschedule our appointment for the same time tomorrow afternoon?
SOPHIE: I'm afraid I've made another appointment for then. I'm sure you're very busy, but do you have time to meet me in the morning?
FRANK: Sure. I'm free after 10. Is 10.30 OK?
SOPHIE: That's great. Thank you very much.
FRANK: No problem.
SOPHIE: Well, I look forward to seeing you tomorrow at 10.30 then.
FRANK: OK ... And I hope your flight isn't delayed too long.
SOPHIE: Me too! Thank you.
FRANK: Bye.
SOPHIE: Bye.

c

1 I'm afraid my flight has been delayed. I'm sorry, but I'm not going to make it to Seoul in time for our appointment.

2 They say two hours, but most of the flights are delayed. I think it's going to be longer than that.

UNIT 9 PART A

3 1

ANNA: Hello, Anna Marsh.
MARTIN: Hello, Anna, it's Martin.
ANNA: Hi, Martin.
MARTIN: I'm just phoning about dates for this advertising meeting ...
ANNA: Oh, yes.

MARTIN: I know the week of the 3rd isn't great for you, but it looks like it will have to be then, sorry. You said you could possibly make the 4th or the 6th?

ANNA: Yes, I can reorganize things and do one of those days, if I know long enough in advance.

MARTIN: OK, thanks. I think Tuesday is the most likely at the moment, starting at 10 o'clock, but I just need to check with Kevin first.

ANNA: That should be fine. Just let me know as soon as you can.

MARTIN: Yes, I will. I'll send an email to confirm. Thanks, Anna. Bye.

ANNA: That's OK. Bye.

2

KEVIN: Kevin Robson.

MARTIN: Hello, Kevin, it's Martin.

KEVIN: Hi, Martin.

MARTIN: I'm just trying to finalize the date of the advertising meeting. Can I double-check dates with you?

KEVIN: Sure.

MARTIN: You said you could possibly make Tuesday 4th or Thursday 6th?

KEVIN: Hold on, I'll just check my diary again ... er, well, things have changed slightly. I can't do Tuesday now, but Wednesday and Thursday are OK.

MARTIN: Ah. Right, let me have a look ... yes, that's OK, we can meet on Thursday 6th then. I'll confirm that in an email to everyone. Thanks, Kevin.

KEVIN: No problem. Bye.

MARTIN: Bye.

UNIT 9 PART B

2

A: What do you think, Paul?

B: I don't think we should ask customers to talk about problems with our products. We want them to look at the positive things, not the negative.

A: I agree, but then how do we get feedback from them?

C: Well, I think you can ask them to make positive suggestions.

A: That's a good idea. So, if this is the kind of feedback we want, we need to decide how to get it.

D: Can I just say something?

A: Sure, go ahead.

D: I think we should send a questionnaire to the cust ...

C: Sorry to interrupt, Mary, but the problem with questionnaires is that most people don't return them.

B: Um ...

A: Paul?

B: I agree. If you ask me, it would be better to ask customers face-to-face when we meet them.

C: Sorry, I didn't quite catch that. What did you say, Paul?

B: Why not ask customers directly when we meet them?

D: I'm not so sure about that. When you ask people face-to-face, they're often not honest in their answers.

A: That's true.

D: Mmm ... how about offering a free gift to customers who return a questionnaire?

A: Good idea. What does everyone think of that?

ALL: Yes ... good idea ... I like that ...

A: OK, good. Shall we just go over what we've said so far? We like the idea of a questionnaire with a free gift ...

UNIT 10 PART A

2

CLIVE: Right, we've just got one week until the meeting with the people from Genus. They've got the programme for the day and the agenda for the meeting ...

GEMMA: Fine. They'll also need our latest product brochures and new trade price lists. Can you send those out now?

CLIVE: Mmm ... maybe we should send the brochures but give them the price list at the meeting.

GEMMA: Yes, you're right. Do you want me to send the brochures? Then perhaps you could organize the price lists.

CLIVE: Sure, no problem. Now, according to the agenda, we're starting with a mini-presentation of the company. Could you do that?

GEMMA: Oh, well, I'm not very good with Powerpoint. I'd rather not, if possible. Could you do it?

CLIVE: OK, if you welcome them and introduce everyone at the start, I'll give the presentation.

GEMMA: Thanks. Are you sure that's OK?

CLIVE: Yeah, that's fine.

GEMMA: So, then we'll work through the agenda. I can lead the discussions about our product range. Do you think you could take over for production times and delivery schedules?

CLIVE: Er, I'd prefer not to talk about processes, if that's OK – you're more familiar with those.

GEMMA: All right, I'll talk about the product range and production times if you discuss delivery schedules. That's more your area, isn't it?

CLIVE: Yes, that would be better. And then it's lunch ...

GEMMA: Oh ... we need to confirm numbers for the restaurant and check if there are any special requests for food, you know, vegetarian and so on ... Would you be able to do that?

CLIVE: Mmm, I might not have time to do that ...

GEMMA: That's OK, I'll get Martine to call or email them and then let the restaurant know.

CLIVE: Good. Now, after lunch we've got the factory tour. We need to arrange that.

GEMMA: I'll do that. I'll ask Chris to lead it. His tour is usually very good ...

CLIVE: Excellent. Then we get down to the real negotiations ...

UNIT 10 PART B

3

1

BUYER: OK. So, we'll place an order for 5,000. But we'd like a 10% discount.

SELLER: Sorry, we can only offer you a 5% discount on this order.

BUYER: That's OK, if you can deliver in two weeks.

SELLER: That's fine.

2

SELLER: We can supply your order but, because you're a new customer, we would like you to pay in advance this time. When you've placed more orders, we can start to look at credit.

BUYER: I'm sorry, but we're not happy about paying everything in advance. We can offer to pay 50%.

SELLER: We'll have to get back to you on that.

3

BUYER: OK. We'll buy 50 sets from you at that price. Can you deliver them by next month?

SELLER: We can deliver by next month, but it will be more expensive. If you pay the extra shipping costs, we'll deliver.

BUYER: That's OK if you can pay for the insurance.

SELLER: Fine.

4

BUYER: We're not sure how many we can sell. If you let us return any not sold within 12 months, we'll take a hundred.

SELLER: Well, we don't normally allow returns. But I could allow you to return items unsold within six months, for this order only.

BUYER: That's fine.

UNIT 11 PART A

3

1

CLERK: Good morning.

CUSTOMER: Morning. I'd like to change US dollars to Swiss francs, please.

CLERK: Certainly. How much do you want to change?

CUSTOMER: 500 dollars.

CLERK: OK. The exchange rate is 1.35 to the dollar, so you'll receive 675 Swiss francs.

CUSTOMER: OK.

2

CLERK: Good afternoon.

CUSTOMER: Hi. Can I change euros to South African rand, please?

CLERK: No problem.

CUSTOMER: What's the exchange rate?

CLERK: It's eight rand to the euro at the moment.

CUSTOMER: OK. I'd like to change 750 euros, please.

CLERK: Thank you. 750 euros buys 6,000 rand, minus 1% commission, that's 60 rand. So you'll receive 5,940 rand. Is that all right?

CUSTOMER: That's fine.

3

CLERK: Can I help you?

CUSTOMER: I'd like to buy Japanese yen, please, with Australian dollars.

CLERK: How much are you changing?

CUSTOMER: What's the exchange rate?

CLERK: 75 yen to the dollar.

CUSTOMER: I'll change 400 dollars, please.

CLERK: OK. You'll receive 30,000 yen.

CUSTOMER: Thank you.

UNIT 11 PART B

2 1

CALL CENTRE WORKER: ... and how would you like to pay for your order?
CUSTOMER: By credit card, please.
CALL CENTRE WORKER: Certainly. Can I have the card number, please?
CUSTOMER: Yes, it's 4929 1234 5678 9012.
CALL CENTRE WORKER: And the expiry date?
CUSTOMER: That's, er, 09/08.
CALL CENTRE WORKER: Thank you. And is the card in your name?
CUSTOMER: Yes, D Buckley, that's right.
CALL CENTRE WORKER: OK. And can I have the security number?
CUSTOMER: I'm sorry. What's that?
CALL CENTRE WORKER: If you look on the back of the card, above your signature, you should see a line of numbers ...
CUSTOMER: Ah, yes ...
CALL CENTRE WORKER: ... and at the end there are three numbers on their own.
CUSTOMER: Yes.
CALL CENTRE WORKER: That's the security number.
CUSTOMER: Ah, OK. That's 923.
CALL CENTRE WORKER: Thank you very much. I'm just waiting for authorization now, then your order can be processed ...

2

CUSTOMER: Good, I think that's everything. Now, how can I pay for such a large order?
SUPPLIER: A direct transfer into our bank is probably the best way.
CUSTOMER: OK. So I'll need some details. What's the account name?
SUPPLIER: Connect Trading Limited.
CUSTOMER: OK, what's the sort code?
SUPPLIER: 44-08-36.
CUSTOMER: And the account number?
SUPPLIER: 98765432.
CUSTOMER: Thanks. Could I have the name and address of your bank, too?
SUPPLIER: Sure. It's ABC Commercial Bank, Marstown Branch. That's at 48, High Street, Marstown, MT8 9PP.
CUSTOMER: Good. Thank you very much. I'll organize that transfer straight away.
SUPPLIER: Thank you. It's been a pleasure doing business with you. We look forward to receiving ...

UNIT 12 PART A

2

A: ... so your company seems to be doing pretty well. What kind of marketing do you use? Do you advertise on TV, for example?
B: We would like to do TV advertising, but it's too expensive. It's a pity though – I'm sure a lot of people enjoy watching the adverts more than the programmes! We use print advertising, especially in magazines. This is successful because it reaches a lot of people – when they open the magazine they can't avoid seeing our adverts. We also use billboard advertising in big cities – everyone says a lot of people see these ads, but I think we need to analyse our billboard advertising. I'm not sure we get many new customers from it. Last year we decided to start direct mail to lists of people, as we can target our market. We already get a good response from that. We've never used telemarketing or sponsorship – we don't think either of these would work for our kind of product – but we're planning to assess our whole marketing strategy next year, to make sure we're using the most effective methods. As you know ...

UNIT 13 PART A

2

SARAH: Come over here, Isaac. There's someone you should meet.
ISAAC: OK.
SARAH: George, can I introduce you to Isaac Bennett? He's a new member. Isaac, this is George Farley. He imports precious stones for a company called Gems Import. Isaac has just arrived in London to market *Financial Review* magazine in Europe.
GEORGE: Really? Good to meet you, Isaac. So, what's *Financial Review* doing here in Europe?
ISAAC: Actually, we're producing a European edition. We've had an office here for six months now and we're about to go into production.
GEORGE: And your job is to get sales under way?
ISAAC: Something like that, yes. That's why I'm here ... at Doing Business, I mean. To try to make contact with some people in the banking and finance sector.

GEORGE: Aha, well ... do you play squash?
ISAAC: Well ... I used to ... but ...
GEORGE: Good, good. There are lots of banking people in the squash ladder. You should join – sure way to meet banking people!
ISAAC: Excellent. Thanks for the tip. Who should I talk to about this squash ladder?
GEORGE: Ah, um, let's see. Ah, Felicity Wells should know ... where is she? ... Ah, oh, there she is. Come on, I'll introduce you.

UNIT 13 PART B

2

GEORGE: Hello, Gems. George Farley speaking.
ISAAC: Hello, George. This is Isaac Bennett. We met at Doing Business a few weeks ago.
GEORGE: Oh, yes, Isaac. How are you? How's it going?
ISAAC: Really well. Sales are good. I made a lot of contacts playing squash, just as you said ...
GEORGE: Oh, good.
ISAAC: ... and I'd like to thank you for your help.
GEORGE: Not at all. Your magazine must be good. You'll have to send me a copy. I'd like to have a look.
ISAAC: Of course, I'd love to. But that's not why I called. I'd like to return the favour. I heard from Felicity that you play golf.
GEORGE: Yes.
ISAAC: I'm playing golf with a friend of mine who manages a department store and I thought you might like to meet her.
GEORGE: That's very kind of you. When are you playing?
ISAAC: Saturday at the Camptown club. We're starting at 1.30.
GEORGE: Well, that sounds great. I'd love to come.
ISAAC: Shall we meet for lunch in the club-house before we start? Say twelve o'clock?
GEORGE: Excellent. I'll see you there then.
ISAAC: Great. Looking forward to it.
GEORGE: OK.
ISAAC: Bye.

UNIT 14 PART A

2

A: OK. Here are the figures and graphs.
B: At last!
A: Yeah. Let's have a look. Er ... OK ... shampoo and haircare products.
B: Sales have gone up. Just as we predicted.
A: Hmm. But they haven't increased as sharply as last year.
B: Well, no. But they have risen a lot.
A: I suppose so. How about sales of bars of soap? Um, there's a chart here somewhere.
B: Here it is. Pretty much the same as last year by the look of it. Mmm, they haven't really moved since 2003. In fact, sales have only gone up slightly since 2001.
A: Hmm. What's this one? Sales have dropped dramatically here.
B: Mouthwash, I think.
A: That's not good. They've fallen sharply in the last two years.
B: I've got the liquid soap market share here. Looks like we're still the market leader, and Raquel is still our biggest competitor, as always. But look at that new company, Gorgeous.
A: Oh, yes. Let's have a look. They've taken 6% of the market share in just one year. We'd better watch out for them!
B: Yes ... what else have we got here then?

UNIT 14 PART B

1

SALES MANAGER:
OK. Now, let's take a look at sales of our soft drinks. First, mineral water. Between 2001 and 2003, sales of mineral water increased from 700,000 to a million dollars. For the last two years, sales haven't really moved. They've been steady at around a million dollars a year. I think sales will go up again in 2006 and 2007, but I don't think there will be a big increase. Sales will probably go up at the same steady rate of increase that we saw between 2001 and 2003. So, by 2007, I hope we can achieve sales of about one and a quarter million.

Now, moving on to fruit juice. Traditionally, this is our strongest seller. From 2001 to 2003, we had sales of about 1.4 million dollars a year, but between 2003 and 2004 sales decreased slightly to 1.2 million. This year, 2005, sales stopped decreasing and held steady at 1.2 million. In the next two years, I don't think we can expect any rapid increases. Our target is to maintain the current level of sales through 2006 and 2007. In fact, I predict sales will increase a little next year, but they probably won't get back to the level of 2001 for quite some time.

UNIT 15 PART A

1 a

CHAIR: OK, er ... next, Naomi Taylor is going to give us a progress report on the new interactive website. Naomi?

NAOMI: Thank you. For those of you who don't know, the interactive website project was started in response to customers who want more information about our services and the option of ordering online. First, I'd like to give a quick outline of the stages of the project. Then I'll explain our progress. We divided our plan into four stages: stage 1, deciding on a website designer; stage 2, working with the designer to plan our website; stage 3, reorganizing the customer services department to deal with the changes and stage 4, building the website. Of course, some of these stages can take place at the same time.

b

NAOMI:

Stage 1 is complete. We talked to several design companies and we've already chosen i2i Media to make the website. They've designed some very impressive websites and they're not too expensive.

Stage 2, planning the site, was started at the same time as stage 1. We wanted to have clear ideas to show the designer immediately. Several of you here today have already given us ideas and we are still looking for more input. So far, we have shown i2i Media what we require and they are still working on a website plan that will meet our requirements. They haven't started on stage 4 yet, building the site.

Stage 3, reorganizing and retraining the customer services department, has already started. Several key personnel have already taken training courses, but we haven't finished yet. We've already bought new software to help with the day-to-day running of the department but we haven't installed it yet, or introduced it to the staff, so they are still using the old system. The project is currently ahead of schedule ...

UNIT 15 PART B

2 MARK:

Good afternoon, everyone, and, er, thanks for coming at the end of a long day of presentations, when the bar probably seems more attractive than me. My name's Mark Plewka. I work for Leading Edge Graphics. My presentation is called 'Communication: The Key to Successful Business', and I hope the title explains itself really – if not, my communication obviously isn't very successful.

Um, my presentation today will be in three main parts: firstly, the reason why communication is important, and why my company decided to focus on communication; secondly, what exactly we did to improve communication within the company; and thirdly, how this model might be applied in other company situations, including possible problems.

OK, to begin, let's look at the importance of communication. I asked a number of company managers three questions about communication in the workplace. As you can see on this transparency, I asked some fairly basic questions, just to find out ...

... which is why it's clear to me that communication is a priority in any workplace. So, let's move on to look at what we did about this. Well, after a series of meetings at all levels within the company ...

... as you can imagine, I could say a lot more about this practical side of things, but time is moving on, so I'll turn to perhaps the most important part for you – how this model might be applied to other situations, possibly including your own, of course ...

... and of course any model will have to be adapted to make it work in different situations. Let me sum up then. Firstly, we looked at the importance of communication in the workplace; secondly, ways of improving communication with specific examples from my own company; and last but by no means least, ways of adapting these solutions to meet the needs of different organizations. I believe that good communication really is the key to successful business. And that brings me to the end of my presentation. Are there any questions?

Acknowledgements

Mark O'Neil would like to thank the long-suffering members of his family in Japan who gave up their time to enable him to work on this project – his children, Talia, Clare, Kieran and Morris and his wife, Soko.

Gareth Knight is grateful to his colleagues at the Department of Linguistics, Srinakharinwirot University and ThaiTESOL for their support and understanding, and to his wife, Sasithorn, for her patience.

Bernie Hayden is indebted to his wife and children for their support and understanding during the many hours spent away from them working on the project.

The authors would like to express most sincere thanks to all the team at Cambridge University Press, in particular, Clare Abbott, Sally Searby, Will Capel and Tony Garside for their unfailing calmness, patience and good humour, and their expert guidance at every stage.

Our thanks also go to Janaka Williams, Debbie Goldblatt, James Hunter and Bridget Green for their expert suggestions and also to Barnaby Pelter for his invaluable input.

The publisher would like to thank the following for permission to reproduce photographs. Sasco Year Planner © Acco Ltd for p. 38(m); Ace Stock for pp. Contents (Units 8 & 13 Headers), 38(tr), pp. Contents (Unit 4 Header), 62, 69(b); Courtesy of Apple for p. 20(tr); Art Directors & TRIP for 14(bl), 20(b3, b4, m, tl); www.baa.com/photolibrary for pp. Contents (Unit 5 Header), 24(br); Bananastock / Alamy for p. 17(l); Courtesy of Brother UK for p. 21(item 6); Courtesy of Canon UK Ltd, image reproduced with kind permission for p. 21(item 2); Corbis for pp. Contents (Unit 14 Header) Doug Chezem, 14(extreme br) Lester Leftkowitz, 17(m) Yang Liu, 21(t) Jose Luis Pelaz Inc, 66 Doug Chezem, 69 Gail Mooney; Carlos Davila / Almay for p. 23(bl); Digital Vision for pp. 7, 72; Dough Boy Ltd for p. 24(t); Education Photos for p. 21(item 4); Ford Motor Company for pp. Contents (Unit 2 Header), 10; Getty Images for pp. Contents (Unit 3 Header) Michael Krasowitz, (Unit 7 Header) Alberto Incrocci, 10 Peter Beavis, 14 Michael Krasowitz, 21(m1) Daly Newton, 23(tr) Rob Brimson, 23(br) Britt Erlanson, 31(item c) Nicholas Russell (item d) Chris M Rogers (item f) Flip Chalfont, 34 Alberto Incrocci, 38(tl) Marcus Lyon, 42 Reza Estakhrianec, 52 Peter Cade; Getty News / AFP for p. 49; Goodshot / Alamy for p. 31(item e); Robert Harding Picture Library for pp. 39(tr), 52; Image100 / Almay for pp. 38(br), 40(bl & m); Imagesource / Alamy for pp. Contents (Units 11 & 15 Headers), 26, 52, 70; Image State / Alamy for p. 17(r), 31(item b); Image State for pp. Contents (Unit 6 Header), 28; Ingram Publishing / Alamy for pp. Contents (Unit 10 Header),16, 48; Initial City Link Ltd for p. 24(bl); Photodisc Green Royalty Free for pp. Contents (Unit 12 Header), 56; Photolibrary.com for pp. 8, 40(r); Powerstock for p. 14(br)Tom Gill; Punchstock / Image100 for p. 14(extreme bl); Punchstock / Image Source for p. 23(tl); Punchstock / Stockbyte for pp. Contents (Unit 1 Header), 6; Reeve Photography for pp. 20(b1 & r), 67, 68; Sony UK Ltd for p. 21(item 5); Zefa for p. 31(item a) A. Inden.

While every effort has been made, it has not been possible to identify the sources of all the material used and in such cases the publishers would welcome information from the copyright owners.

Picture Research by Kevin Brown

Illustrations by Kamae Design